VOGUE® KNITTING

STITCHIONARY™

The Ultimate Stitch Dictionary from the Editors of Vogue® Knitting Magazine

volume one
knit & purl

VOGUE® KNITTING
STITCHIONARY™

The Ultimate Stitch Dictionary from the Editors of Vogue® Knitting Magazine

volume one
knit & purl

Sixth&Spring Books
233 Spring Street
New York, New York 10013

Editorial Director
Trisha Malcolm

Book Editor
Carla Scott

Art Director
Chi Ling Moy

Graphic Designer
Sheena Thomas

Instructions Editor
Lisa Buccellato

Copy Editors
Lisa Buccellato
Charlotte Parry

Yarn Editor
Veronica Manno

Book Division Manager
Erica Smith

Production Manager
David Joinnides

President and Publisher, Sixth&Spring Books
Art Joinnides

5   7   9   10   8   6
Fifth printing, 2007
Manufactured in China

Library of Congress Control Number: 2005929994
ISBN: 1-931543-77-1
ISBN-13: 978-1-931543-77-4

Photo Credits:
Jack Deutsch (Front cover and back cover)
Tom Wool (p. 9)
Paul Amato (pp. 49, 141, 107)

contents

We dedicate this book to all the incredibly talented designers and knitters who have contributed over the years to making *Vogue Knitting* such a unique magazine.

When I think back to 1982—the comeback of *Vogue Knitting*—it seems like yesterday. I remember the press arriving for the launch party at our offices in SoHo. Knitting was having a renaissance, and it was all the news. I was asked to knit a sweater for a newscaster from the local network. She even wore it several times on-air after that. I was thrilled to see that knitting was so current, and to know I was a part of it.

During my many years with the magazine I have always wanted to create the ultimate stitch book, but it was never the right time. Here we are in the twenty-first century and knitting is more popular than ever before. What could be a better time than now?

Together with Trisha Malcolm, we decided to look through all the past issues of *Vogue Knitting* and extract all of those special (and basic) stitch patterns that have been pub-lished in the magazine, beginning with the first issue. The task was overwhelming, but it was so satisfying to remember all the good times (and heartaches) that went into putting these issues together.

We realized that putting all of the stitches in one book would have made the book much too big. So we decided instead to begin with three separate volumes. This is our first volume: *Knit & Purl*. From the most basic of stitches to the most com-plex, this volume gives over 250 permuta-tions of the knit and purl stitch, along with yarn overs, to yield the most interesting patterns. Our next two volumes, *Cables* and *Colorwork*, will be just as inspiring.

You might ask yourself: What can I do with all of these stitches? To that I say: have fun and get creative! After years of knitting endless numbers of swatches, there is nothing more satisfying than to learn a new technique or try a new stitch. Experimenting with yarns—their endless colors and textures—gives you a whole new perspective on the art of knitting. You can take a plain Stockinette stitch sweater, pick a new stitch that you like, and combine them to make a fabulous, unique garment. Or, you can try making various swatches of the patterns that you like, and sew them all together for a long scarf or a textured afghan.

We hope that this book, and the next two to come, will inspire and excite all those who knit (or want to learn how). Let your cre-ativity flow!

Carla Scott

victorian ferns p. 103

how to use this book

This first volume of the *Vogue Knitting Stitchionary* is divided into four chapters: Knit & Purl, Lace, Traveling, and Unusual. Within each chapter, the stitches are arranged in order of difficulty, from the easiest to the hardest.

All of the instructions use the *Vogue Knitting* style, with standard knitting abbreviations and easy-to-understand terminology. See page 182 for the illustrations of the most commonly-used techniques and explanations of the abbreviations. If there is a specific technique that is exclusive to a particular swatch, then the explanation for that technique is located within the instructions for that swatch.

We have used one yarn for all of the swatches: Lana Grossa Cool Wool 2000. This DK weight, 100% wool yarn is perfect for showing the detail of the stitches in a crisp, clean manner. We have tried to keep the swatches the same size, and in most cases we show at least two repeats of the pattern, both in stitches and in rows. We have used size 6 (4mm) needles to knit the swatches. Note that if you use a different weight or textured yarn, the resulting look of the stitch may be different than what we show.

Selvages have been added to the side edges, usually in garter stitch. This is to keep the edges somewhat flat. We have steamed them a little to get out the worst of the curling, but did not want to steam the texture out of the stitch. So when you see some of the edges not completely flat, it was on purpose. It also resembles what your actual knitting will look like. Sometimes extra rows are added to the beginning and end as well. These extra stitches and rows are NOT in the instructions. Therefore, when it says "a multiple of 6 sts plus 2" this will not include the selvage stitches.

Just remember, always make a gauge swatch with the yarn you are using for the project. This will make you familiar with the pattern stitch and you will know if that particular stitch works well with the yarn you are using. And please note that some stitches are continuous, with pattern repeats, and some are panels that can be inserted into a design or combined with other stitches.

knit & purl

1 seed stitch

(multiple of 2 sts plus 1)
Row 1 (RS) K1, *p1, k1; rep from * to end.
Rep row 1.

2 condo knitting garter stripes

(any number of sts)
Rows 1–6 With 2 strands of yarn held tog, knit.
Rows 7 and 9 (RS) With 1 strand of yarn, knit.
Rows 8 and 10 With 1 strand of yarn, purl.
Rep rows 1–10.

1

2

3 purl ridges

(worked over an odd number of sts)
Row 1 (RS) Knit.
Rows 2 and 4 Purl.
Row 3 K1, *p1, k1; rep from * to end.
Rep rows 1–4.

4 simple slip stitch

(multiple of 4 sts plus 3)
Row 1 (RS) K1, *sl 1, k3; rep from *, end sl 1, k1.
Row 2 Purl.
Rep rows 1 and 2.

knit & purl

3

4

5 slip stitch and yarn over ridges

(any number of sts)
Row 1 (WS) K1, *wyif sl 1 purlwise, yo; rep from *, end k1.
Row 2 K1, *k next st and yo tog tbl; rep from *, end k1.
Rows 3 and 5 K1, p to last st, k1.
Rows 4 and 6 Knit.
Rep rows 1–6.

6 moss stitch

(multiple of 4 sts)
Rows 1 (RS) *K2, p2; rep from * to end.
Rows 2 and 3 *P2, k2; rep from * to end.
Row 4 *K2, p2; rep from * to end.
Rep rows 1–4.

5

6

7 sugar cubes

(multiple of 8 sts plus 1)
Rows 1 and 5 (RS) Knit.
Rows 2, 4, 6 and 8 K the knit sts and p the purl sts.
Row 3 K1, *p2, k6; rep from * to end.
Row 7 K5, *p2, k6; rep from * to last 4 sts, end p2, k2.
Rep rows 1–8.

8 garter ridge rib

(multiple of 3 sts)
Rows 1 and 3 (RS) K1, *p1, k2; rep from *, end p1, k1.
Row 2 K2, *p2, k1; rep from *, end k2.
Row 4 Knit.
Rep rows 1–4.

knit & purl

7

8

(multiple of 4 sts plus 2)

Row 1 (RS) *K1, p1; rep from * to end.

Row 2 *K3, p1; rep from *, end k2.

Row 3 P2, *k1, p3; rep from * to end.

Row 4 Rep row 1.

Row 5 *K1, p3; rep from *, end p1.

Row 6 K1, p1, *k3, p1; rep from * to end.

Rep rows 1–6.

(multiple of 3 sts plus 2)

Row 1 (RS) P2, *k1, p2; rep from * to end.

Row 2 *K2, p1; rep from *, end k2.

Rows 3, 5, 7, 9, 11 and 13 Rep row 1.

Rows 4, 6, 8, 10, 12 and 14 Rep row 2.

Rows 15–30 Knit.

Rep rows 1–30.

9

10

11 wide rib

(multiple of 10 sts plus 5)
Row 1 (RS) P5, *k5, p5; rep from * to end.
Row 2 K the knit sts and p the purl sts.
Rep rows 1 and 2.

12 wide slip stitch

(multiple of 10 sts plus 3)
Row 1 (WS) K1, *p1, k9; rep from *, end p1, k1.
Row 2 P1, *wyib sl 1 purlwise, p9; rep from *,
end wyib sl 1 purlwise, p1.
Rep rows 1 and 2.

knit & purl

11

12

(over an odd number of sts)
Row 1 (RS) K1, *p1, k1; rep from * to end.
Row 2 Purl.
Rep rows 1 and 2.

(multiple of 5 sts plus 2)
Row 1 (RS) K3, *p1, k4; rep from *, end last rep k3.
Row 2 *P2, k3; rep from *, end p2.
Rep rows 1 and 2.

13

14

15 brioche rib

(over an odd number of sts)
K1-b (Knit 1 in row below)
Row 1 (WS) Knit.
Row 2 *K1, k1-b; rep from *, end k1 (mark this row as RS).
Row 3 K2, *k1-b, k1; rep from *, end k1.
Rep rows 2 and 3.

16 slip stitch brioche rib

(cast on even number of sts, worked over multiple of 3 sts plus 2)
Row 1 (RS) K1, *yo, sl 1, k1; rep from *, end k1.
Row 2 K1, *yo, sl 1, k2tog; rep from *, end k1.
Rep row 2.

knit & purl

15

16

17 ridge stitch

(multiple of 3 sts plus l)
Row 1 (RS) K1, *p2, k1; rep from * to end.
Row 2 Knit.
Rep rows 1 and 2.

18 broken slip stitch

(multiple of 4 sts plus 3)
Row 1 (WS) *K3, p1; rep from *, end k3.
Row 2 *K3, sl 1; rep from *, end k3.
Rows 3–10 Rep rows 1 and 2 four times.
Row 11 K5, p1, *k3, p1; rep from *, end k5.
Row 12 K5, sl 1, *k3, sl 1; rep from *, end k5.
Rows 13–20 Rep rows 11 and 12 four times.
Rep rows 1–20.

17

18

19 broken rib with twist

(multiple of 4 sts)

RT (right twist) K2tog but do not drop from LH needle, knit first st again and drop both sts from LH needle.

Row 1 (RS) *K2, p2; rep from * to end.

Rows 2–8 K the knit sts and p the purl sts.

Row 9 *RT, p2; rep from * to end.

Rows 10–18 K the knit sts and p the purl sts.

Row 19 *P2, k2; rep from * to end.

Rows 20–26 K the knit sts and p the purl sts.

Row 27 *P2, RT; rep from * to end.

Rows 28–36 K the knit sts and p the purl sts.

Rep rows 1–36.

20 herringbone rib

(multiple of 13 sts plus 7)

RT (right twist) K2tog leaving sts on LH needle and k first st again

Row 1 (RS) [P1, k1] 3 times, p1, *RT 3 times, [p1, k1] 3 times, p1; rep from * to end.

Rows 2 and 4 *[K1, p1] 3 times, k1, p6; rep from *, end [k1, p1] 3 times, k1.

Row 3 [P1, k1] 3 times, p1, *k1, RT twice, k1, [p1, k1] 3 times, p1; rep from * to end.

Rep rows 1–4.

knit & purl

21 mock cable wide rib

(multiple of 13 sts plus 8)

Row 1 (WS) P8, *k1, p3, k1, p8; rep from * to end.

Row 2 K8, *p1, skip 2 sts, k 3rd st on LH needle, k 2nd st, then k first st, then sl all 3 sts off LH needle, p1, k8; rep from * to end.

Rep rows 1 and 2.

22 zigzag rib

(multiple of 10 sts plus 5)

3-st RC (3 st right cross) Sl 2 sts to cn and hold to back, k1, k2 from cn.

3-st LC (3 st left cross) Sl 1 st to cn and hold to front, k2, k1 from cn.

Row 1 (RS) *P2, k1, p2, k1 tbl, 3-st RC, k1 tbl; rep from *, end p2, k1, p2.

Rows 2 and 4 *K2, p1, k2, wyif sl 1, p3, wyif sl 1; rep from *, end k2, p1, k2.

Row 3 *P2, k1, p2, k1 tbl, 3-st LC, k1 tbl; rep from *, end p2, k1, p2.

Rep rows 1–4.

21

22

knit & purl

(multiple of 5 sts plus 3)

LT (left twist) With RH needle behind first st on LH needle, insert RH needle knitwise into second st, k this st and leave on needle, k the first st, sl both sts off needle tog.

Row 1 (RS) *P3, LT; rep from *, end p3.

Row 2 K3, *p2, k3; rep from * to end.

Rep rows 1 and 2.

(multiple of 25 sts)

RT (right twist) K2 tog leaving sts on needle, k first st, sl both sts from needle.

LT (left twist) Insert RH needle in back of second st on LH needle and k st tbl, leave sts on needle, k2 tog tbl.

Row 1 (RS) *P2, k1 tbl, p1, k1 tbl, p2, k2 tbl, p2, k1 tbl, p1 (center st), k1 tbl, p2, k2 tbl, p2, k1 tbl, p1, k1 tbl, p2; rep from *, end.

Row 2 *K2, p1 tbl, k1, p1 tbl, k2, p2 tbl, k2, p1 tbl, k1 (center st), p1 tbl, k2, p2 tbl, k2, p1 tbl, k1, p1 tbl, k2; rep from *, end.

Row 3 *P2, k1 tbl, p1, k1 tbl, p2, RT, p2, k1 tbl, p1 (center st), k1 tbl, p2, LT, p2, k1 tbl, p1, k1 tbl, p2; rep from *, end.

Row 4 *K2, p1 tbl, k1, p1 tbl, k2, p2 tbl, k2, p1 tbl, k1 (center st), p1 tbl, k2, p2 tbl, k2, p1 tbl, k1, p1 tbl, k2; rep from *, end.

Rep rows 1 4.

23

24

25 twisted stitch rib

(multiple of 3 sts plus 2)

LT (left twist) (worked on RS rows) With RH needle behind work, k 2nd st on LH needle through back lp (tbl), leave st on needle; then k first st through front lp; sl both sts from needle.

RT (right twist) (worked on WS rows) P 2nd st on LH needle, leave st on needle; p first st; sl both sts from needle.

Row 1 (RS) *LT, p1; rep from *, end LT.

Row 2 *RT, k1; rep from *, end RT.

Rep rows 1 and 2.

26 basketweave rib

(multiple of 10 sts plus 2)

Row 1 (RS) *P2, k4, p2, k2; rep from *, end p2.

Row 2 K the knit sts and p the purl sts.

Row 3 *P2, k2, p2, k4; rep from *, end p2.

Row 4 Rep row 2.

Rep rows 1–4.

25

26

27 small diamond brocade

(multiple of 12 sts plus 5)

Row 1 (RS) *K8, p1, k3; rep from *, end k5.

Row 2 P5, *p2, k1, p1, k1, p7; rep from * to end.

Rows 3 and 7 *K2, [p1, k3] twice, p1, k1; rep from *, end k2, p1, k2.

Rows 4 and 6 [P1, k1] twice, p1, *k1, p5, [k1, p1] 3 times; rep from * to end.

Row 5 *P1, k3, p1, k7; rep from *, end p1, k3, p1.

Row 8 Rep row 2.

Rep rows 1–8.

28 diamond brocade

knit & purl

(multiple of 12 sts plus 5)

Rows 1 and 5 (RS) *K8, p1, k3; rep from *, end k5.

Rows 2, 4 and 6 P5, *p2, k1, p1, k1, p7; rep from * to end.

Row 3 *K6, p1, k3, p1, k1; rep from *, end k5.

Row 7 *K2, [p1, k3] twice, p1, k1; rep from *, end k2, p1, k2.

Row 8 [P1, k1] twice, p1, *k1, p5, [k1, p1] 3 times; rep from * to end.

Row 9 *P1, k3, p1, k7; rep from *, end, p1, k3, p1.

Row 10 Rep row 8.

Row 11 Rep row 7.

Row 12 Rep row 2.

Rep rows 1–12.

27

28

(multiple of 8 sts)

Row 1 (RS) *[K3, p1] twice; rep from * to end.

Row 2 *[P3, k1] twice; rep from * to end.

Row 3 * K1, p1, k3, p1, k2; rep from * to end.

Row 4 *P1, k1, p3, k1, p2; rep from * to end.

Rows 5 and 7 Knit.

Row 6 *K1, p3, k4; rep from * to end.

Rows 8 and 10 Purl.

Row 9 *P4, k3, p1; rep from * to end.

Row 11 *P1, k5, p2; rep from * to end.

Row 12 *K3, p5; rep from * to end.

Row 13 *K4, p3, k1; rep from * to end.

Row 14 *P2, k3, p3; rep from * to end.

Row 15 *K2, p3, k3; rep from * to end.

Rows 16 and 18 Purl.

Row 17 *[K1, p1] 4 times; rep from * to end.

Row 19 *K2, p1, k3, p1, k1; rep from * to end.

Row 20 *P2, k1, p3, k1, p1; rep from * to end.

Row 21 *[P1, k3] twice; rep from * to end.

Row 22 *[K1, p3] twice; rep from * to end.

Rows 23 and 25 Knit.

Row 24 *K1, p3, k4; rep from * to end.

Rows 26 and 28 Purl.

Row 27 *P4, k3, p1; rep from * to end.

Row 29 *K2, p3, k3; rep from * to end.

Row 30 *P2, k3, p3; rep from * to end.

Row 31 *K4, p3, k1; rep from * to end.

Row 32 *K3, p5; rep from * to end.

Row 33 *P1, k5, p2; rep from * to end.

Rows 34 and 36 Purl.

Row 35 *[K1, p1] 4 times.

Rep rows 1–36.

29

(multiple of 12 sts)

Row 1 (RS) *K6, p6; rep from * to end.

Row 2 *K6, p6; rep from * to end.

Rows 3 and 4 *P1, k5, p5, k1; rep from * to end.

Rows 5 and 6 *K1, p1, k4, p4, k1, p1; rep from * to end.

Rows 7 and 8 *P1, k1, p1, k3, p3, k1, p1, k1; rep from * to end.

Rows 9 and 10 *[K1, p1] twice, k2, p2, [k1, p1] twice; rep from * to end.

Rows 11 and 12 *[P1, k1] 6 times; rep from * to end.

Rows 13 and 14 *[K1, p1] 6 times; rep from * to end.

Rows 15 and 16 *[P1, k1] twice, p2, k2, [p1, k1] twice.; rep from * to end

Rows 17 and 18 *[K1, p1] twice, p2, k2, [p1, k1] twice; rep from * to end.

Rows 19 and 20 *P1, k1, p4, k4, p1, k1; rep from * to end.

Rows 21 and 22 *K1, p5, k5, p1; rep from * to end.

Rows 23 and 24 *P6, k6; rep from * to end.

Rows 25 and 26 *P5, k1, p1, k5; rep from * to end.

Rows 27 and 28 *P4, [k1, p1] twice, k4; rep from * to end.

Rows 29 and 30 *P3, [k1, p1] 3 times, k3, rep from * to end.

Rows 31 and 32 *P2, [k1, p1] 4 times, k2; rep from * to end.

Rows 33 and 34 *[P1, k1] 6 times; rep from * to end.

Rows 35 and 36 *[K1, p1] 6 times; rep from * to end.

Rows 37 and 38 *K2, [p1, k1] 4 times, p2; rep from * to end.

Rows 39 and 40 *K3, [p1, k1] 3 times, p3; rep from * to end.

Rows 41 and 42 *K4, [p1, k1] twice, p4; rep from * to end.

Rows 43 and 44 *K5, p1, k1, p5; rep from * to end.

Rep rows 1–44.

30

31 seed stitch basketweave

(multiple of 10 sts plus 1)

Rows 1 and 9 (RS) K4, *p1, k1, p1, k7; rep from *, end k4.

Rows 2, 4, 6 and 8 P3, *[k1, p1] twice, k1, p5; rep from *, end p3.

Rows 3, 5 and 7 K2, *[p1, k1] 3 times, p1, k3; rep from *, end k2.

Rows 10 and 12 Purl.

Row 11 Knit.

Rows 13 and 21 K1, p1, *k7, p1, k1, p1; rep from * end last rep p1, k1.

Rows 14, 16, 18 and 20 K1, p1, k1, *p5, [k1, p1] twice, k1; rep from *, end k1, p1, k1.

Rows 15, 17 and 19 [K1, p1] twice, *k3, [p1, k1,] 3 times, p1; rep from *, end [p1, k1] twice.

Rows 22 Purl.

Row 23 Knit.

Row 24 Purl.

Rep rows 1–24.

32 simple basketweave

(multiple of 8 sts)

Row 1 (RS) Knit.

Rows 2–6 *K4, p4; rep from * to end.

Row 7 Knit.

Rows 8–12 *P4, k4; rep from * to end.

Rep rows 1–12.

33 pie crust basketweave

(multiple of 8 sts plus 10)
Rows 1 and 3 (WS) K4, *p2, k6; rep from *, end p2, k4.
Row 2 P4, *k2, p6; rep from *, end k2, p4.
Row 4 Knit.
Rows 5 and 7 K8, *p2, k6; rep from *, end p2, k8.
Row 6 P8, *k2, p6; rep from *, end k2, p8.
Row 8 Knit.
Rep rows 1–8.

34 waffle rib

(multiple of 5 sts)
Row 1 (RS) Knit.
Row 2 Purl.
Rows 3 and 5 *K2, p3; rep from * to end.
Rows 4 and 6 *K3, p2; rep from * to end.
Rep rows 1–6.

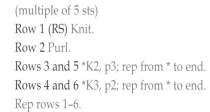

knit & purl

33

34

(multiple of 12 sts)

Rows 1, 3, 7 and 9 (RS) *P2, k4; rep from * to end.

Rows 2, 4, 8 and 10 *P4, k2; rep from * to end.

Row 5 *P8, k4; rep from * to end.

Row 6 *P4, k8; rep from * to end.

Row 11 P2, *k4, p8; rep from *, end p6.

Row 12 K6, *p4, k8; rep from *, end k2.

Rep rows 1–12.

(multiple of 18 sts plus 18)

Row 1 (RS) K6, *p2, k2, p2, k12; rep from *, end k6.

Row 2 K4, *[p2, k2] twice, p2, k8; rep from *, end k4.

Row 3 P4, *[k2, p2] twice, k2, p8; rep from *, end p4.

Row 4 P6, *k2, p2, k2, p12; rep from *, end p6.

Rows 5–8 Rep rows 1–4.

Row 9 Knit.

Row 10 P1, k2, p2, *p10, [k2, p2] twice; rep from *, end k2, p1.

Row 11 K1, p2, k2, *p8, [k2, p2] twice, k2; rep from *, end k2, p2, k1.

Row 12 P1, k2, p2, *k8, [p2, k2] twice, p2; rep from *, end p2, k2, p1.

Row 13 K1, p2, *k12, p2, k2, p2; rep from *, end p2, k1.

Rows 14–17 Rep rows 10–13.

Row 18 Purl.

Rep rows 1–18.

35

36

37 bamboo basketweave

(multiple of 18 sts)
Row 1 (RS) Knit.
Rows 2 and 3 Purl.
Row 4 Knit.
Rows 5, 9 and 13 *P3, k6, p3, k6; rep from * to end.
Rows 6, 10 and 14 *P6, k3, p6, k3; rep from * to end.
Rows 7 and 11 *P3, k6, p9; rep from * to end.
Rows 8 and 12 *K9, p6, k3; rep from * to end.
Rows 15, 18 and 19 *Purl.
Rows 16, 17 and 20 Knit.

Rows 21, 25 and 29 *P3, k6, p3, k6; rep from * to end.
Rows 22, 26 and 30 *P6, k3, p6, k3; rep from * to end.
Rows 23 and 27 *P12, k6; rep from * to end.
Rows 24 and 28 *P6, k12; rep from * to end.
Row 31 Purl.
Row 32 Knit.
Rep rows 1–32.

38 basketweave blocks

knit & purl

(multiple of 18 sts, knit with 2 strands held tog)
RT (right twist) K into back loop of 2nd st on LH needle, then k into back loop of first st on LH needle, sl both sts off needle.
LT (left twist) Working behind first st on LH needle, k into back loop of 2nd st, then k into back loop of first st, sl both sts off needle.
Row 1 (RS) *LT, k7; rep from * to end.
Rows 2 and 4 *K7, p11; rep from * to end.
Row 3 *RT, k7; rep from * to end.
Rows 5–12 Rep rows 1–4 twice.
Row 13 *LT, k7; rep from * to end.
Rows 14 and 16 *P9, k7, p2; rep from * to end.
Row 15 *RT, k7; rep from * to end.
Rows 17–24 Rep rows 13–16 twice.
Rep rows 1 24.

37

38

(multiple of 8 sts)

Row 1 (RS) *K1, p1, k1, p5; rep from * to end.

Row 2 and all WS rows K the knit sts and p the purl sts.

Row 3 K1, p1, *k5, p1, k1, p1; rep from *, end k5, p1.

Row 5 K1, *p5, k1, p1, k1; rep from *, end p5, k1, p1.

Row 7 *K5, p1, k1, p1; rep from * to end.

Row 9 P4, *k1, p1, k1, p5; rep from *, end [k1, p1] twice.

Row 11 K3, *p1, k1, p1, k5; rep from *, end p1, k1, p1, k2.

Row 13 P2, *k1, p1, k1, p5; rep from *, end k1, p1, k1, p3.

Row 15 K1, *p1, k1, p1, k5; rep from *, end p1, k1, p1, k4.

Row 16 Rep row 2.

Rep rows 1–16.

(multiple of 4 sts plus 2)

Rows 1, 3 and 5 (WS) P2, *[k into back and front of st] twice, p2; rep from * to end.

Rows 2, 4 and 6 K2, *[p2tog] twice, k2; rep from * to end.

Rows 7, 9 and 11 [K into back and front of st] twice, *p2, [k into back and front of st] twice; rep from * to end.

Rows 8, 10 and 12 [P2tog] twice, *k2, [p2tog]twice; rep from * to end.

Rep rows 1–12.

39

40

knit & purl

(worked over 15 sts on a background of St st)

Row 1 (RS) K6, p1, k1, p1, k6.

Row 2 P5, k2, p1, k2, p5.

Row 3 K4, p2, k3, p2, k4.

Row 4 P3, k2, p5, k2, p3.

Row 5 K2, p2, k2, p1, k1, p1, k2, p2, k2.

Row 6 P1, k2, p2, k2, p1, k2, p2, k2, p1.

Row 7 K1, p1, k2, p2, k3, p2, k2, p1, k1.

Row 8 P3, k2, p5, k2, p3.

Row 9 K2, p2, k2, p1, k1, p1, k2, p2, k2.

Row 10 P2, k1, p2, k2, p1, k2, p2, k1, p2.

Row 11 K4, p2, k3, p2, k4.

Row 12 P3, k2, p5, k2, p3.

Row 13 K3, p1, k2, p1, k1, p1, k2, p1, k3.

Row 14 P5, k2, p1, k2, p5.

Row 15 K4, p2, k3, p2, k4.

Row 16 P4, k1, p5, k1, p4.

Row 17 K6, p1, k1, p1, k6.

Row 18 P5, k2, p1, k2, p5.

Row 19 K5, p1, k3, p1, k5.

Row 20 Purl.

Row 21 K6, p1, k1, p1, k6.

Row 22 P6, k1, p1, k1, p6.

Row 23 K7, p1, k7.

Row 24 P7, k1, p7.

Rep rows 1–24.

41

(multiple of 27 sts)

TT (throw three) Bring yarn from back to front and wrap around RH needle 3 times, end with yarn at back.

Drop TT (drop throw three) Sl 3 TT of previous row from LH needle to front of work for bow twist.

Tie Bow After Drop TT row has been worked, insert point of needle into loops to remove slack. Tie loops on RS.

Rows 1 and 3 (RS) P3, [k1 tbl, p1, k1 tbl, p6] twice, k1 tbl, p1, k1 tbl, p3.

Rows 2 and 4 K3, [p1 tbl, k1, p1 tbl, k6] twice, p1 tbl, k1, p1 tbl, k3.

Row 5 P3, k1 tbl, p1, [k1 tbl, p7] twice, k1 tbl, p1, k1 tbl, p3.

Row 6 K3, p1 tbl, k1, [p1 tbl, k7] twice, p1 tbl, k1, p1 tbl, k3.

Row 7 P3, [k1 tbl, p1, k1 tbl, p6], twice, k1 tbl, p1, k1tbl, p3.

Row 8 K3, [p1 tbl, k1, p1 tbl, k6] twice, p1 tbl, k1, p1 tbl, k3.

Row 9 P3, k1 tbl, p1, k1 tbl, p5, [k1 tbl, p1] twice, k1 tbl, p5, k1 tbl, p1, k1 tbl, p3.

Row 10 K3, p1 tbl, k1, p1 tbl, k5, [p1 tbl, k1] twice, p1 tbl, k5, p1 tbl, k1, p1 tbl, k3.

Row 11 P3, k1 tbl, p1, k1 tbl, p4, [k1 tbl, p1] 3 times, k1 tbl, p4, k1 tbl, p1, k1 tbl, p3.

Row 12 K3, p1 tbl, k1, p1 tbl, k4, [p1 tbl, k1] 3 times, p1 tbl, k4, p1 tbl, k1, p1 tbl, k3.

Row 13 P3, k1 tbl, p1, k1 tbl, p3, [k1 tbl, p1] 4 times, k1 tbl, p3, k1 tbl, p1, k1 tbl, p3.

Row 14 K3, p1 tbl, k1, p1 tbl, k3, [p1 tbl, k1] 4 times, p1 tbl, k3, p1 tbl, k1, p1 tbl, k3.

Rows 15 and 16 Rep rows 7 and 8.

Rows 17 and 18 Rep rows 5 and 6.

Rows 19 and 20 Rep rows 3 and 4.

Row 21 P3, k1 tbl, p1, k1 tbl, p6, [k1 tbl, TT] twice, k1 tbl, p6, k1 tbl, p1, k1 tbl, p3.

Row 22 K3, p1 tbl, k1, p1 tbl, k6, [p1 tbl, drop TT] twice, p1 tbl, k6, p1 tbl, k1, p1 tbl, k3. Tie bow on next row.

Row 23 and 24 P3, [k1 tbl, p1, k1 tbl, p6] twice, k1 tbl, p1, k1 tbl, p3.

Row 25 and 26 K3, [p1 tbl, k1, p1 tbl, k6] twice, p1 tbl, k1, p1 tbl, k3.

Rep rows 1–26.

42

knit & purl

(worked over 9 sts)

Row 1 (RS) K8, p1.

Row 2 P1, k1, p7.

Row 3 K6, p1, k1, p1.

Row 4 [P1, k1] twice, p5.

Row 5 K4, [p1, k1] twice, p1.

Row 6 [P1, k1] 3 times, p3.

Row 7 K2, [p1, k1] 3 times, p1.

Rows 8, 9 and 10 [P1, k1] 4 times, p1.

Row 11 K2, [p1, k1] 3 times, p1.

Row 12 [P1, k1] 3 times, p3.

Row 13 K4, [p1, k1] twice, p1.

Row 14 [P1, k1] twice, p5.

Row 15 K6, p1, k1, p1.

Row 16 P, k1, p7.

Row 17 K8, p1.

Row 18 P9.

Row 19 P1, k8.

Row 20 P7, k1, p1.

Row 21 P1, k1, p1, k6.

Row 22 P5, [k1, p1] twice.

Row 23 [P1, k1] twice, p1, k4.

Row 24 P3, [k1, p1] 3 times.

Row 25 [P1, k1] 3 times, p1, k2.

Row 26 P1, [k1, p1] 4 times, k1.

Row 27 [P1, k1] 4 times, p1.

Row 28 P1, [k1, p1] 4 times.

Row 29 [P1, k1] 3 times, p1, k2.

Row 30 P3, [k1, p1] 3 times.

Row 31 [P1, k1] twice, p1, k4.

Row 32 P5, [k1, p1] twice.

Row 33 P1, k1, p1, k6.

Row 34 P7, k1, p1.

Row 35 P1, k8.

Row 36 Purl.

Rep rows 1–36.

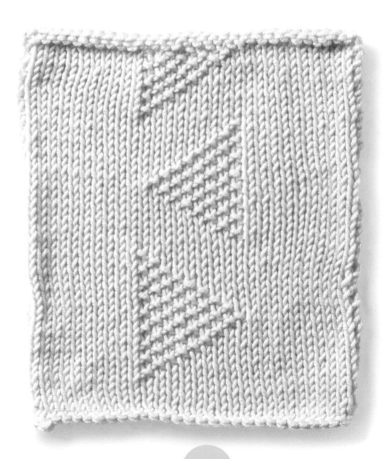

(worked over 25 sts)

Rows 1, 3, 5 and 7 (RS) P1, k1, [k1, p1] 10 times, k2, p1.

Rows 2, 4 and 6 [K1, p1] 12 times, k1.

Row 8 [K1, p1] 6 times, p2, [k1, p1] 5 times, k1.

Row 9 P1, k1, [k1, p1] 4 times, k5, [p1, k1] 4 times, k1, p1.

Row 10 [K1, p1] 5 times, p2, k1, p3, [k1, p1] 4 times, k1.

Row 11 P1, k1, [k1, p1] 3 times, k3, [p1, k1] twice, k2, [p1, k1] 3 times, k1, p1.

Row 12 [K1, p1] 4 times, p2, [k1, p1] 3 times, p2, [k1, p1] 3 times, k1.

Row 13 P1, k1, [k1, p1] twice, k3, [p1, k1] 4 times, k2, [p1, k1] twice, k1, p1.

Row 14 [K1, p1] 3 times, p2, [k1, p1] 5 times, p2, [k1, p1] twice, k1.

Row 15 P1, k2, p1, k3, [p1, k1] 6 times, k2, p1, k2, p1.

Row 16 [K1, p1] twice, p2, [k1, p1] 7 times, p2, k1, p1, k1.

Row 17 P1, k4, [p1, k1] 8 times, k3, p1.

Row 18 K1, p3, [k1, p1] 9 times, p2, k1.

Row 19–28 Rep rows 1 and 2 five times.

Rep rows 1–28.

44

45 slip stitch waffle

(multiple of 5 sts plus 4)
Row 1 (WS) *K4, yo, k1; rep from *, end k4.
Row 2 *K4, wyib sl 1 purlwise dropping the yo of previous row; rep from *, end k4.
Rows 3 and 5 *P4, sl 1; rep from *, end p4.
Rows 4 and 6 *K4, sl 1; rep from *, end k4.
Rep rows 1–6.

46 eyelet herringbone

(multiple of 9 sts plus 2)
RT (right twist) Skip next st and insert needle into 2nd st through front lp, draw up a lp, then insert needle into skipped st and let both sts fall from needle.
Row 1 and all WS rows K2, *p7, k2; rep from * to end.
Row 2 *P2, RT twice, k2tog, yo, k1; rep from *, end p2.
Row 4 *P2, k1, RT, k2tog, yo, RT; rep from *, end p2.
Row 6 *P2, RT, k2tog, yo, RT, k1; rep from *, end p2.
Row 8 *P2, k1, k2tog, yo, RT twice; rep from *, end p2.
Row 10 *P2, k2tog, yo, RT twice, k1; rep from *, end p2.
Row 12 *P2, k1, RT 3 times; rep from *, end p2.
Rep rows 1–12.

knit & purl

45

46

47 float stitch blocks

(multiple of 6 sts plus 2)

Rows 1, 3 and 5 (RS) K1, *k3, wyif sl 3; rep from *, end k1.

Row 2 and all WS rows K1, purl across to last st, end k1.

Rows 7, 9 and 11 K1, *wyif sl 3, k3; rep from *, end k1.

Row 12 K1, purl across to last st, end k1.

Rep rows 1–12.

48 linen ridge stitch

(multiple of 2 sts)

Row 1 (RS) Purl.

Row 2 (WS) K1, *wyif sl 1 , k1; rep from * to last st, end k1.

Row 3 Purl.

Row 4 K1, *k1, wyif sl 1; rep from * end k1.

Rep rows 1–4.

47

48

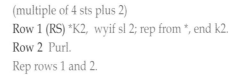

knit & purl

(multiple of 4 sts)

PT (**purl twist**) P2 tog leaving sts on LH needle, insert RH needle from back between sts just worked and p the first st again, sl both st from needle tog.

Rows 1 and 3 (WS) Purl.

Row 2 *K2, PT; rep from * to end.

Row 4 *PT, k2; rep from * to end.

Rep rows 1–4.

(multiple of 4 sts plus 2)

Row 1 (RS) *K2, wyif sl 2; rep from *, end k2.

Row 2 Purl.

Rep rows 1 and 2.

49

50

(worked over an even number of sts)

Note Pattern requires 2 different needle sizes, 4 sizes apart.

Cast on with larger needles.

Row 1 (RS) With smaller needles, knit.

Row 2 With larger needles, purl.

Row 3 With smaller needles, k1 (selvage st), *insert tip of RH needle through first st as to purl and around to k the foll st and leave on needle, then k the first st tbl, sl both sts to RH needle for one cross-stitch; rep from *, end k1 (selvage st).

Rep rows 2 and 3.

(multiple of 3 sts plus 1)

Row 1 (RS) K1, *yo, sl 1, k2, pass sl st over 2 k sts; rep from * to end.

Row 2 P1, *yo, sl 1, p2, pass sl st over 2 p sts; rep from * to end.

Rep rows 1 and 2.

51

52

knit & purl

53 diagonal float stitch

(multiple of 6 sts)
Row 1 and all WS rows Purl.
Row 2 (RS) *Wyif sl 3, k3; rep from * to end.
Row 4 K1, *wyif sl 3, k3; rep from *, end k2.
Row 6 K2, *wyif sl 3, k3; rep from *, end k1.
Row 8 *K3, wyif sl 3; rep from * to end.
Row 10 Wyif sl 1, *k3, wyif sl 3; rep from *, end wyif sl 2.
Row 12 Wyif sl 2, *k3, wyif sl 3; rep from *, end wyif sl 1.
Rep rows 1–12.

54 scale pattern

(multiple of 6 sts)
Row 1 (WS) *Yo, k3, pass the yo over the k3, wyib sl 3 purl-wise; rep from * to end.
Row 2 Knit.
Row 3 *Yo, k3, pass the yo over the k3, p3; rep from * to end.
Row 4 *K1, with RH needle lift thread in front of sl sts of row 1, place on LH needle and knit it with the next st, k4; rep from * to end.
Row 5 *Wyib, sl 3 purlwise, bring yarn to front and yo, k3, pass the yo over the k3; rep from * to end.
Row 6 Knit.
Row 7 *P3, yo, k3, pass yo the over the k3; rep from * to end.
Row 8 *K4, with RH needle lift thread in front of sl sts of row 5, place on LH needle and knit it with the next st, k1; rep from * to end.
Rep rows 1–8.

53

54

55 diagonal slip stitch

(multiple of 4 sts plus 5)

Row 1 (WS) Purl.

Row 2 K1, *sl 1, k3; rep from * to end.

Row 3 *P3, sl 1; rep from *, end p1.

Row 4 K1, *drop next sl st off LH needle to front of work, k2, pick up dropped st and k it, k1; rep from * to end.

Row 5 Purl.

Row 6 K3, *k2, sl 1, k1; rep from *, end k2.

Row 7 P2, *p1, sl 1, p2; rep from *, end p3.

Row 8 K3, *sl next 2 sts, drop next sl st off LH needle to front, place 2 sl sts back on LH needle, pick up dropped st and k it, k3; rep from *, end k2.

Rep rows 1–8.

56 quilted stockinette

(multiple of 6 sts plus 3)

Q1 (quilt 1) Insert RH needle under the loose strand at front of work and k next st, pulling out st under strand.

Rows 1, 3, 5, and 7 (WS) Purl.

Row 2 K2, *sl 5, k1; rep from *, end k1.

Row 4 K4, *Q1, k5; rep from * to last 5 sts, Q1, k4.

Row 6 K1, sl 3, *k1, sl 5; rep from * to last 5 sts, k1, sl 3, k1.

Row 8 K1, *Q1, k5; rep from * to last 2 sts, Q1, k1.

Rep rows 1–8.

55

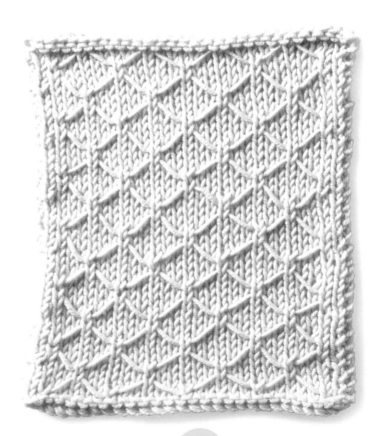

56

knit & purl

(multiple of 8 sts plus 7)

Row 1 (RS) K1, *sl 1, k4, pass sl st over the 4 k sts, p3; rep from *, end k1.

Row 2 K1, p1, *k1, k1 st under running thread between st just worked and next st, k1, p5; rep from *, end p1, k1.

Row 3 K2, *p3, k5; rep from *, end p3, k2.

Row 4 K1, p1, *k3, p5; rep from *, end k3, p1, k1.

Row 5 K2, *p3, wyib sl 1, k4, pass sl st over 4 k sts; rep from *, end p3, k2.

Row 6 K1, *p5, k1, k1 under running thread, k1; rep from *, end p5, k1.

Row 7 K1, *k5, p3; rep from *, end k6.

Row 8 K1, *p5, k3, rep from *, end p5, k1.

Rep rows 1–8.

(worked over an even number of sts)

Row 1 (RS) *K1, sl 1; rep from * to end.

Rows 2 and 6 Slip the slipped sts and p the purl sts.

Rows 3 and 7 Knit.

Rows 4 and 8 Purl.

Row 5 *Sl 1, k1; rep from * to end.

Rep rows 1–8.

57

58

(multiple of 4 sts plus 3)

Row 1 (RS) K3, *sl 1, k3; rep from * to end.

Rows 2, 4, 6 and 8 K3, *p1, k3; rep from * to end.

Rows 3, 5 and 7 P3, *sl 1, p3; rep from * to end.

Row 9 Rep row 1.

Row 10 Purl.

Rep rows 1–10.

(multiple of 10 sts plus 6)

Row 1 (RS) *K8, p2; rep from *, end k6.

Row 2 P5, k1, *k2, p7, k1; rep from * to end.

Row 3 *P2, k6, p2; rep from *, end p2, k4.

Row 4 P3, k3, *k2, p5, k3; rep from * to end.

Row 5 *P4, k4, p2; rep from *, end p4, k2.

Row 6 P1, k5, *k2, p3, k5; rep from * to end.

Row 7 *P6, k2, p2; rep from *, end p6.

Row 8 Rep row 6.

Row 9 Rep row 5.

Row 10 Rep row 4.

Row 11 Rep row 3

Row 12 Rep row 2.

Rep rows 1–12.

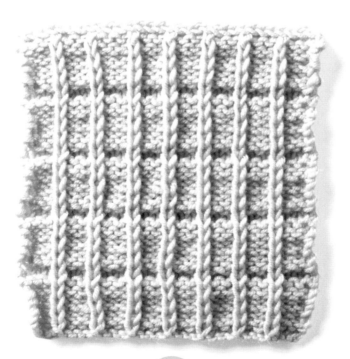

59

60

61 small mock brocade pleats

(multiple of 7 sts)
Row 1 (RS) *P6, k1; rep from * to end.
Row 2 *P2, k5; rep from * to end.
Row 3 *P4, k3; rep from * to end.
Row 4 *P4, k3; rep from * to end.
Row 5 *P2, k5; rep from * to end.
Row 6 *P6, k1; rep from * to end.
Rep rows 1–6.

62 alternating twists

(multiple of 9 sts plus 2)
Row 1 (WS) K2, *p3, k1, p3, k2; rep from * to end.
Row 2 *P2, wyib sl 1, k2, p1, k2, wyib sl 1; rep from *, end p2.
Row 3 K2, *wyif sl 1, p2, k1, p2, wyif sl 1, k2; rep from * to end.
Row 4 *P2, drop sl st off needle to front of work, k2, pick up dropped st and k it, p1, wyib sl next 2 sts, drop sl st off needle to front of work, sl same 2 sts back to LH needle, pick up dropped st and k it; rep from *, end k2.
Row 5 K2, *p3, k1, p3, k2; rep from * to end.
Row 6 *P2, k3, p1, k3; rep from *, end p2.
Rep rows 1–6.

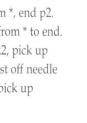

knit & purl

61

62

(multiple of 4 sts plus 1)

Row 1 (RS) *P1, k3; rep from *, end p1.

Rows 2 and 4 *K1, p3; rep from *, end k1.

Row 3 *P1, skip 2 sts, k third st on LH needle, k first st, k second st, then sl these 3 sts off LH needle; rep from *, end p1.

Rep rows 1–4.

(multiple of 25 sts)

Row 1 (RS) *P9, k4, p12; rep from * to end.

Row 2 *[P3, k1] 3 times, p4, k1, [p3, k1] twice; rep from * to end.

Row 3 *[P1, k3] twice, p1, 4-st RC, [p1, k3] 3 times; rep from * to end.

Row 4 Rep row 2.

Rep row 1–4.

63

64

knit & purl

(multiple of 6 sts plus 1)

S2KP Slip 2 sts tog, k1, pass 2 sl sts over k1.

Row 1 (RS) Knit.

Row 2 Knit.

Rows 3, 4 and 5 Purl.

Row 6 Knit.

Row 7 P1, *p2, k1, p3; rep from * to end.

Row 8 *K3, p1, k2; rep from *, end k1.

Row 9 P2tog, *p1, M1, k1, M1, p1, p3tog; rep from *, end p2tog.

Row 10 *K2, p3, k1; rep from *, end k1.

Row 11 P2tog, *M1, k3, M1, p3tog; rep from *, end p2tog.

Row 12 *K1, p5; rep from *, end k1.

Row 13 P1, *M1 p-st, ssk, k1, k2tog, M1 p-st, p1; rep from * to end.

Row 14 *K2, p3, k1; rep from *, end k1.

Row 15 P1, *p1, M1 p-st, SK2P, M1 p-st, p2; rep from * to end.

Row 16 *K3, p1, k2; rep from *, end k1.

Rep rows 1–16.

(multiple of 9 sts plus 1)

Note When working pat st, sl all sl-sts purlwise.

Row 1 (RS) K1, *p2, k3, p2, k2; rep from * to end.

Row 2 P2, *k2, p3, k2, p2; rep from *, end p1.

Row 3 K1, *p2, bring yarn to back, sl 1, k2tog, psso, p2, k2; rep from * to end.

Row 4 P2, *k2, (p1, k1, p1) in same st, k2, p2; rep from *, end p1.

Rep rows 1–4.

(multiple of 4 sts plus 2)

Row 1 (RS) K1, *k1, sl 1 purlwise, k1, yo, pass the slipped st over the k st and yo, k1; rep from *, end k1.

Row 2 Purl.

Rep rows 1 and 2.

66

67

knit & purl

(multiple of 18 sts)

Row 1 (RS) *K1, p2, k3, p2, k5, p1, k4; rep from * to end.

Row 2 *P3, k1, p1, k1, p3, k2, p5; k2; rep from * to end.

Row 3 *K1, [p2, k3] twice, [p1, k1] twice, p1, k2; rep from * to end.

Row 4 *P3, k1, p1, k1, p5, k2, p1, k2, p2; rep from * to end.

Row 5 *K3, p1, k1, p1, k5, [p1, k1] twice, p1, k2; rep from * to end.

Row 6 *[P1, k1] 4 times, p3, k2, p1, k2, p2; rep from * to end.

Row 7 *K1, p2, k3, p2, [k1, p1] 5 times; rep from * to end.

Row 8 *[P1, k1] 4 times, p1, k2, p5, k2; rep from * to end.

Row 9 *K1, p2, k3, p2, k10; rep from * to end.

Row 10 *K9, p2, k2, p1, k2, p2; rep from * to end.

Row 11 *K3, p1, k1, p1, k12; rep from * to end.

Row 12 *K9, p2, k2, p1, k2, p2; rep from * to end.

Rep rows 1–12.

(multiple of 8 sts plus 2)

FS (front slip) Wyib sl 1 purlwise, drop sl st off needle to front of work, sl same p st back to LH needle, pick up dropped st and k it, p1.

BS (back slip) Drop sl st off needle to front of work, p1, pick up dropped st and k it.

Preparation row (WS) K1, *k3, p2, k3; rep from *, end k1.

Rows 1 and 3 P1, *p3, k2, p3; rep from *, end p1.

Row 2 and all WS rows K the knit sts and wyif sl the p sts .

Row 5 P1, *p2, FS, BS, p2; rep from *, end p1.

Row 7 P1, *p1, FS, p2, BS, p1; rep from * end p1.

Row 9 P1, *FS, p4, BS; rep from *, end p1.

Rows 11 and 13 P1, *k1, p6, k1; rep from *, end p1.

Row 15 P1, *BS, p4, FS; rep from *, end p1.

Row 17 P1, *p1, BS, p2, FS, p1; rep from *, end p1.

Row 19 P1, *p2, BS, FS, p2; rep from *, end p1.

Row 20 Rep row 2.

Rep rows 1–20.

69

lace

70 very simple eyelet

(multiple of 8 sts plus 7)
Row 1 (RS) Knit.
Row 2 and all WS rows Purl.
Row 3 *K6, yo, k2tog; rep from *, end k7.
Row 5 Knit.
Row 7 K2, *yo, k2tog, k6; rep from *, end k3.
Row 8 Purl .
Rep rows 1–8.

71 simple eyelet

(multiple of 4 sts plus 3)
Rows 1 and 5 (RS) Knit.
Row 2 and all WS rows Purl.
Row 3 K1, *k2tog, yo, k2; rep from *, end k2.
Row 7 K1, *k2, ssk, yo; rep from *, end k2.
Row 8 Purl.
Rep rows 1–8.

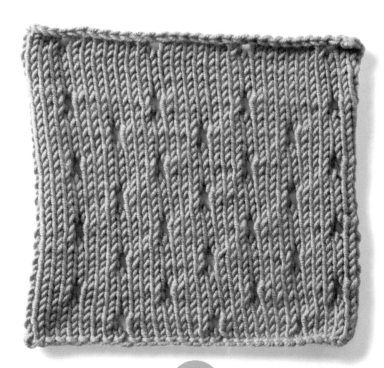

70

71

72 eyelet ridges

(multiple of 2 sts plus 1)
Row 1 (RS) Knit.
Rows 2 and 4 Knit.
Row 3 *K2tog, yo; rep from *, end k1.
Rows 5 to 14 Work in St st.
Rep rows 1–14.

73 simple eyelet diamonds

(multiple of 8 sts)
Row 1 and all WS rows Purl.
Row 2 Knit.
Row 4 K3, *yo, ssk, k6; rep from *, end k3.
Row 6 K1, *k2tog, yo, k1, yo, ssk, k3; rep from *, end k2.
Row 8 Rep row 4.
Row 10 Knit.
Row 12 K7; rep from * of row 4, end k1.
Row 14 K5; rep from * of row 6, end k3.
Row 16 Rep row 12.
Rep rows 1–16.

72

73

74 eyelet hyacinths

(multiple of 32 sts)

Row 1 (RS) Knit.

Row 2 and all WS rows Purl.

Row 3 *K3, RT, k1, LT, k24; rep from * to end.

Row 5 *K2, RT, k2tog, yo, k1, LT, k23; rep from * to end.

Row 7 *K1, RT, k2tog, yo, k1, yo, SKP, LT, k10, k2tog, yo, k10; rep from * to end.

Row 9 *RT, k1, k2tog, yo, k1, yo, SKP, k1, LT, k8, k2tog, yo, k1, yo, SKP, k8; rep from * to end.

Row 11 *K3, k2tog, yo, k1, yo, SKP, k24; rep from * to end.

Row 13 *K4, k2tog, yo, k26; rep from * to end.

Rows 15, 17, 19 and 21 Knit.

Row 23 *K19, RT, k1, LT, k8; rep from * to end.

Row 25 *K18, RT, k2tog, yo, k1, LT, k7; rep from * to end.

Row 27 *K4, k2tog, yo, k11, RT, k2tog, yo, k1, yo, SKP, LT, k6; rep from * to end.

Row 29 *K3, k2tog, yo, k1, yo, SKP, k8, RT, k1, k2tog, yo, k1, yo, SKP, k1, LT, k5; rep from * to end.

Row 31 *K19, k2tog, yo, k1, yo, SKP, k8; rep from * to end.

Row 33 *K20, k2tog, yo, k10; rep from * to end.

Rows 35, 37 and 39 Knit.

Row 40 Purl.

Rep rows 1–40.

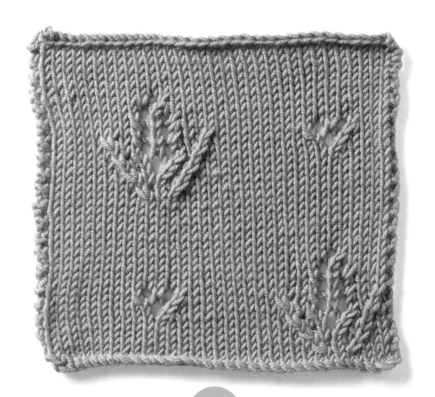

75 leaves of grass

(multiple of 11 sts)

Row 1 (RS) *Yo, ssk, k9; rep from * to end.

Row 2 and all WS rows Purl.

Row 3 *K1, yo, ssk, k8; rep from * to end.

Row 5 *K2, yo, ssk, k4, k2tog, yo, k1; rep from * to end.

Row 7 *K3, yo, ssk, k2, k2tog, yo, k2; rep from * to end.

Row 9 *K6, k2tog, yo, k3; rep from * to end.

Row 11 *K5, k2tog, yo, k4; rep from * to end.

Row 12 Purl.

Rep rows 1–12.

76 eyelet blocks

(multiple of 8 sts plus 3)

Row 1 (RS) K2, *p3, k5; rep from *, end k1.

Row 2 P1, *p5, k3; rep from *, end p2.

Row 3 K2, *p1, yo, p2tog, k5; rep from *, end k1.

Row 4 P1, *p5, k3; rep from *, end p2.

Row 5 K2, *p3, k5; rep from *, end k1.

Row 6 Purl.

Row 7 K1, *k5, p3; rep from *, end k2.

Row 8 P2, *k3, p5; rep from *, end p1.

Row 9 K1, *k5, p1, yo, sl2-k1-p2sso; rep from *, end k2.

Row 10 P2, *k3, p5; rep from *, end p1.

Row 11 K1, *k5, p3; rep from *, end k2.

Row 12 Purl.

Rep rows 1–12.

lace

75

76

77 faggoted panel

(multiple of 20 sts plus 4)

Rows 1, 3 and 5 (RS) *P4, [k1 tbl, k1] twice, [yo, p2tog] 4 times, [k1, k1 tbl] twice; rep from *, end p4.

Rows 2, 4 and 6 *K4, [p1 tbl, k1] twice, [yo, p2tog] 4 times, [k1, p1 tbl] twice; rep from *, end k4.

Rows 7, 9 and 11 *P4, k1 tbl, k1, k1 tbl, p1, k8, p1, k1 tbl, k1, k1 tbl; rep from *, end p4.

Rows 8, 10 and 12 *K4, [p1 tbl, k1] twice, p8, [k1, p1 tbl] twice; rep from *, end k4.

Rep rows 1–12.

78 tiny eyelet rib

(multiple of 5 sts plus 3)

Row 1 (RS) *P1, k1 tbl, p1, k2; rep from *, end p1, k1 tbl, p1.

Row 2 K1, p1 tbl, k1, *p2, k1, p1 tbl, k1; rep from * to end.

Row 3 *P1, k1 tbl, p1, k1, yo, k1; rep from *, end p1, k1 tbl, p1.

Row 4 K1, p1 tbl, k1, *p3, k1, p1 tbl, k1; rep from * to end.

Row 5 *P1, k1 tbl, p1, k3, pass the 3rd st on RH needle over the center 2 sts; rep from *, end p1, k1 tbl, p1.

Rep rows 2–5.

77

78

79 lace rib

(multiple of 6 sts plus 2)
Rows 1 and 3 (WS) *P2, k1; rep from *, end p2.
Row 2 *K2, p1, yo, ssk, p1; rep from *, end k2.
Row 4 *K2, p1, k2tog, yo, p1; rep from *, end k2.
Rep rows 1–4.

80 drop stitch pattern

(multiple of 8 sts plus 2)
Preparation row (RS) *P2, k1, yo, k1, p2, k2; rep from *, end p2.
Rows 1, 3 and 5 (WS) *K2, p2, k2, p3; rep from *, end k2.
Rows 2 and 4 *P2, k3, p2, k2; rep from *, end p2.
Row 6 *P2, k1, drop next st off needle and unravel to the yo 6 rows below, k1, p2, k1, yo, k1; rep from *, end p2.
Rows 7, 9 and 11 *K2, p3, k2, p2; rep from *, end k2.
Rows 8 and 10 *P2, k2, p2, k3; rep from *, end p2.
Row 12 *P2, k1, yo, k1, p2, k1, drop next st off needle and unravel 6 rows down, k1; rep from *, end p2.
Rep rows 1–12.

lace

79

80

81 alternating eyelets

(worked over 14 sts)
Rows 1 and 3 (WS) Purl.
Row 2 K1, yo, k1, k2tog, k1, yo, k2tog, SKP, yo, k1, SKP, k1, yo, k1.
Row 4 K2, k2tog, yo, k1, yo, k2tog, SKP, yo, k1, yo, SKP, k2.
Rep rows 1–4.

82 eyelet chains

(worked over14 sts)
4-st FYC (4-st front yarn over cable)
Sl 2 sts to cn and hold to *front*, k2, then yo, k2tog from cn.
Row 1 (RS) K3, p2, 4-st FYC, p2, k3.
Row 2 and all WS rows P3, k2, p2, yo, p2tog tbl, k2, p3.
Rows 3, 5, 7 and 9 K3, p2, k2, yo, k2tog, p2, k3.
Row 10 Rep row 2.
Rep rows 1–10.

81

82

83 pair of eyelets

(multiple of 16 sts plus 12)

Rows 1, 3, 5, 7 (WS) P3 K1, *k5, p3, k4, p4; rep from *, end k5, p3.

Rows 2 and 6 K3, *yo, k2tog, SKP, yo, p4, yo, SKP, k1, p5; rep from *, end p1, k3.

Rows 4 and 8 K3, p5, *yo, k2tog, SKP, yo, p4, k1, yo, k2tog, p5; rep from *, end p1, k3.

Rep rows 1–8.

84 horseshoe crab

(multiple of 12 sts plus 3)

Row 1 (RS) K1, k2tog, yo, *k2, yo, k1, sl 1-k2tog-psso, k1, yo, k2, yo, sl 1-k2tog-psso, yo; rep from * to last 12 sts, k2, yo, k1, sl 1-k2tog-psso, k1, yo, k2, yo, SKP, k1.

Row 2 Purl.

Row 3 K1, k2tog, yo, *k3, yo, sl 1-k2tog-psso, yo; rep from * to last 6 sts , k3, yo, SKP, k1.

Row 4 Purl.

Rep rows 1–4.

83

84

85 granite relief stitch

(multiple of 2 sts)
Row 1 (RS) Knit.
Row 2 K2tog across row.
Row 3 K into the front and back of each st.
Row 4 Purl.
Rep rows 1–4.

86 diagonal cluster lace

(multiple of 3 sts)
Row 1 (WS) Purl .
Row 2 K2, *yo, k3, pass first of the 3 knit sts over the 2nd and 3rd sts; rep from *, end k1.
Row 3 Purl .
Row 4 K1, *k3, pass first of the 3 knit sts over the 2nd and 3rd sts, yo; rep from *, end k2.
Rep rows 1–4.

85

86

87 daisy pattern

(multiple of 4 sts plus 1)

DS (daisy stitch)

P3tog, but do not let the 3 sts fall from LH needle, wind yarn around RH needle over top and back to front again, then p the same 3 sts tog again and let fall from needle.

Rows 1 and 3 (RS) Knit.

Row 2 K1, *work DS over next 3 sts, k1; rep from * to end.

Row 4 K1, p1, k1, *work DS over next 3 sts, k1; rep from *, end p1, k1.

Rep rows 1–4.

88 purse stitch

(worked over an even number of sts)

Row 1 K1, *yo, ssk; rep from *, end k1.

Rep row 1.

lace

87

88

89 faggoting pattern

(multiple of 3 sts)
Row 1 (RS) *K1, yo, k2tog; rep from * to end.
Rep row 1.

90 mesh pattern 1

(worked over an even number of sts)
Row 1 (RS) *Yo, k2tog; rep from * to end.
Rows 2 and 4 Purl.
Row 3 *SKP, yo; rep from * to end.
Rep rows 1–4.

89

90

91 mesh pattern 2

(worked over an even number of sts)
Row 1 (RS) K1, *yo, k2tog; rep from *, end k1.
Rows 2 and 4 Purl.
Row 3 K1, *k2tog, yo; rep from *, end k1.
Rep rows 1–4.

92 cat's eye

(multiple of 4 sts)
Row 1 (RS) K4, *yo twice, k4; rep from * to end.
Row 2 P2, *p2tog, [p1, k1] in double yo, p2tog; rep from *, to last 2 sts, p2.
Row 3 K2, yo, *k4, yo twice; rep from * to last 6 sts, k4, yo, k2.
Row 4 P3, *[p2tog] twice, [p1, k1] in double yo; rep from * to last 7 sts, [p2tog] twice, p3.
Rep rows 1–4.

91

92

93 open trellis

(multiple of 4 sts plus 2)

RT (right twist) k2tog leaving sts on LH needle, then insert RH needle from front between 2 sts knitted tog and k first st again, then sl both sts from needle tog – right twist (RT)

LT (left twist) with RH needle behind LH needle, skip 1 st and k 2nd st on LH needle tbl, then insert RH needle into back lps of both skipped st and 2nd st and k2tog tbl

Row 1 (RS) P2, *p2; rep from * to end.

Row 2 K2, *p2, k2; rep from * to end.

Row 3 P1, *k2tog, yo twice, SKP; rep from *, end p1.

Row 4 P2, *[k1, p1] into double yo, p2; rep from * to end.

Row 5 K2, *p2, ; rep from *, end p2, k2.

Row 6 P2, *k2, p2; rep from * to end.

Row 7 P1, yo, *SKP, k2tog, yo twice; rep from *, end SKP, k2tog, yo, p1.

Row 8 K2, *p2, [k1,p1] into double yo; rep from *, end p2, k2.

Rep rows 1–8.

94 rivulet

(multiple of 3 sts plus 4)

Row 1 K2, *sl 1-k2tog-psso, yo twice; rep from *, end k2.

Row 2 K2, *[p1, k1] into double yo, p1; rep from *, end k2.

Row 3 Knit.

Rep rows 1–3.

93

94

(multiple of 12 sts plus 4)

P2tog-tbl P2 sts tog through back lps.

P3tog-tbl P2tog, then sl the resulting st back to LH needle, with RH needle pass the next st from LH needle over this st, then sl this st back to RH needle.

Row 1 (RS) K2, *k2tog, yo, k2, k2tog, yo twice, ssk, k2, yo, ssk; rep from *, end k2.

Row 2 K2, *k1, p2, p2tog tbl, yo, [k1, p1]) into double yo, yo, p2tog, p2, k1; rep from *, end k2.

Row 3 K2, *k2, k2tog, yo, k4, yo, ssk, k2; rep from *, end k2.

Row 4 P2, *p3tog tbl, yo, p1, yo, p4, yo, p1, yo, p3tog; rep from *, end p2.

Row 5 K2, *yo, ssk, k2, yo, ssk, k2tog, yo, k2, k2tog, yo; rep from *, end k2.

Note The yo's at the beg and end form a yo twice.

Row 6 P2, *p1, yo, p2tog, p2, k2, p2, p2tog tbl, yo, k1; rep from *, end p2.

Note The p1 at the beg and the k1 at the end form a k1, p1 into double yo of row 5, as on row 2.

Row 7 K2, *k2, yo, ssk, k4, k2tog, yo, k2; rep from *, end k2.

Row 8 P2, *p2, yo, p1, yo, p3tog, p3tog-tbl, yo, p1, yo, p2, rep from *, end p2.

Rep rows 1–8.

96 diagonal planes

(multiple of 11 sts)

Row 1 (RS) *SKP, k6, yo, p3; rep from * to end.

Row 2 *K3, p8; rep from * to end.

Rep rows 1 and 2.

97 eyelet pleats

(multiple of 8 sts)

Row 1 (RS) *K6, k2tog, yo; rep from * to end.

Row 2 *K1, p7; rep from * to end.

Row 3 *K5, k2tog, yo, p1; rep from * to end.

Row 4 *K2, p6; rep from * to end.

Row 5 *K4, k2tog, yo, p2; rep from * to end.

Row 6 *K3, p5; rep from * to end.

Row 7 *K3, k2tog, yo, p3; rep from * to end.

Row 8 *K4, p4; rep from * to end.

Row 9 *K2, k2tog, yo, p4; rep from * to end.

Row 10 *K5, p3; rep from * to end.

Row 11 *K1, k2tog, yo, p5; rep from * to end.

Row 12 *K6, p2; rep from * to end.

Row 13 *K2tog, yo, p6; rep from * to end.

Row 14 *K7, p1; rep from * to end.

Rep rows 1–14.

(multiple of 12 sts)

Row 1 (RS) * K2, p4, k2tog, yo, k4; rep from * to end.

Row 2 * P6, k4, p2; rep from * to end.

Row 3 *K1, p4, k2tog, yo, k5; rep from * to end.

Row 4 *P7, k4, p1; rep from * to end.

Row 5 *P4, k2tog, yo, k6; rep from * to end.

Row 6 *P8, k4; rep from * to end.

Row 7 *K3, yo, ssk, p4, k3; rep from * to end.

Row 8 *P3, k4, p5; rep from * to end.

Row 9 *K4, yo, ssk, p4, k2; rep from * to end.

Row 10 *P2, k4, p6; rep from * to end.

Row 11 *K5, yo, ssk, p4, k1; rep from * to end.

Row 12 *P1, k4, p7; rep from * to end.

Row 13 *K2, p4, k2tog, yo, k4; rep from * to end.

Row 14 *P6, k4, p2; rep from * to end.

Row 15 *K1, p4, k2tog, yo, k5; rep from * to end.

Row 16 *P7, k4, p1; rep from * to end.

Row 17 *P4, k2tog, yo, k6; rep from * to end.

Row 18 *P8, k4; rep from * to end.

Row 19 *K3, yo, ssk, p4, k3; rep from * to end.

Row 20 *P3, k4, p5; rep from * to end.

Row 21 *K4, yo, ssk, p4, k2; rep from * to end.

Row 22 *P2, k4, p6; rep from * to end.

Row 23 *K5, yo, ssk, p4, k1; rep from * to end.

Row 24 *P1, k4, p7; rep from * to end.

Rep rows 1–24.

98

99 tulip leaves

(worked over 49 sts)

Row 1 (RS) P1, k1, p2, [k1 tbl, p1] twice, p2, k7, p2, [k1 tbl, p1] twice, p4, [k1 tbl, p1] twice, p1, k7, p3, [k1 tbl, p1] twice, p1, k1, p1.

Row 2 K1, p1, k2, [p1 tbl, k1] twice, k2, p7, k2, [p1 tbl, k1] twice, k4, [p1 tbl, k1] twice, k1, p7, k3, [p1 tbl, k1] twice, k1, p1, k1.

Row 3 [K1, p1] twice, [k1 tbl, p1] twice, p2, k5, SKP, p2, [k1 tbl, p1] twice, [p1, yo] twice, p2, [k1 tbl, p1] twice, p1, k2tog, k5, p3, [k1 tbl, p1] twice, k1, p1, k1.

Row 4 [P1, k1] twice, [p1 tbl, k1] twice, k2, p6, k2, [p1 tbl, k1] twice, [k1, p1] twice, k2, [p1 tbl, k1] twice, k1, p6, k3, [p1 tbl, k1] twice, p1, k1, p1.

Row 5 P1, k1, p2, [k1 tbl, p1] twice, p2, k4, SKP, p2, [k1 tbl, p1] twice, p1, yo, k1, p1, k1, yo, p2, [k1 tbl, p1] twice, p1, k2tog, k4, p3, [k1 tbl, p1] twice, p1, k1, p1.

Row 6 K1, p1, k2, [p1 tbl, k1] twice, k2, p5, k2, [p1 tbl, k1] twice, [k1, p2] twice, k2, [p1 tbl, k1] twice, k1, p5, k3, [p1 tbl, k1] twice, k1, p1, k1.

Row 7 [K1, p1] twice, [k1 tbl, p1] twice, p2, k3, SKP, p2, [k1 tbl, p1] twice, p1, yo, k2, p1, k2, yo, p2, [k1 tbl, p1] twice, p1, k2tog, k3, p3, [k1 tbl, p1] twice, k1, p1, k1.

Row 8 [P1, k1] twice, [p1 tbl, k1] twice, k2, p4, k2, [p1 tbl, k1] twice, k1, p3, k1, p3, k2, [p1 tbl, k1] twice, k1, p4, k3, [p1 tbl, k1] twice, p1, k1, p1.

Row 9 P1, k1, p2, [k1 tbl, p1] twice, p2, k2, SKP, p2, [k1 tbl, p1] twice, p1, yo, k3, p1, k3, yo, p2, [k1 tbl, p1] twice, p1, k2tog, k2, p3, [k1 tbl, p1] twice, p1, k1, p1.

Row 10 K1, p1, k2, [p1 tbl, k1] twice, k2, p3, k2, [p1 tbl, k1] twice, k1, p4, k1, p4, k2, [p1 tbl, k1] twice, k1, p3, k3, [p1 tbl, k1] twice, k1, p1, k1.

Row 11 [K1, p1] twice, [k1 tbl, p1] twice, p2, k1, SKP, p2, [k1 tbl, p1] twice, p1, yo, k4, p1, k4, yo, p2, [k1 tbl, p1] twice, p1, k2tog, k1, p3, [k1 tbl, p1] twice, k1, p1, k1.

Row 12 [P1, k1] twice, [p1 tbl, k1] twice, k2, p2, k2, [p1 tbl, k1] twice, k1, p5, k1, p5, k2, [p1 tbl, k1] twice, k1, p2, k3, [p1 tbl, k1] twice, p1, k1, p1.

Row 13 P1, k1, p2, [k1 tbl, p1] twice, p2, SKP, p2, [k1 tbl, p1] twice, p1, yo, k5, p1, k5, yo, p2, [k1 tbl, p1] twice, p1, k2tog, p3, [k1 tbl, p1] twice, p1, k1, p1.

Row 14 K1, p1, k2, [p1 tbl, k1] twice, k2, p1, k2, [p1 tbl, k1] twice, k1, p6, k1, p6, k2, [p1 tbl, k1] twice, k1, p1, k3, [p1 tbl, k1] twice, k1, p1, k1.

Row 15 [K1, p1] twice, [k1 tbl, p1] twice, p1, p2tog, p2, [k1 tbl, p1] twice, p1, yo, k6, p1, k6, yo, p2, [k1 tbl, p1] twice, p1, p2tog, p2, [k1 tbl, p1] twice, k1, p1, k1.

Row 16 [P1, k1] twice, [p1 tbl, k1] twice, k4, [p1 tbl, k1] twice, [k1, p7], k2, [p1 tbl, k1] twice, k4, [p1 tbl, k1] twice, p1, k1, p1.

Row 17 P1, k1, p2, [k1 tbl, p1] twice, p4, [k1 tbl, p1] twice, [p1, k7], p2, [k1 tbl, p1] twice, p4, [k1 tbl, p1] twice, p1, k1, p1.

Row 18 K1, p1, k2, [p1 tbl, k1] twice, k4, [p1 tbl, k1] twice, [k1, p7], k2, [p1 tbl, k1] twice, k4, [p1 tbl, k1] twice, k1, p1, k1.

Row 19 [K1, p1] twice, [k1 tbl, p1] twice, p4, [k1 tbl, p1] twice, k2tog, k6, yo, p1, yo, k6, SKP, p1, [k1 tbl, p1] twice, p4, [k1 tbl, p1] twice, k1, p1, k1.

Row 20 [P1, k1] twice, [p1 tbl, k1] twice, k4, [p1 tbl, k1] twice, p7, p1 tbl, k1, p1 tbl, p7, k1, [p1 tbl, k1] twice, k4, [p1 tbl, k1] twice, p1, k1, p1.

Row 21 P1, k1, p2, [k1 tbl, p1] twice, p4, k1 tbl, p1, k1 tbl, k2tog, k6, yo, p3, yo, k6, SKP, k1 tbl, p1, k1 tbl, p5, [k1 tbl, p1] twice, p1, k1, p1.

Row 22 K1, p1, k2, [p1 tbl, k1] twice, k4, p1 tbl, k1, p1 tbl, p7, p1 tbl, k3, p1 tbl, p7, p1 tbl, k1, p1 tbl, k5, [p1 tbl, k1] twice, k1, p1, k1.

Row 23 [K1, p1] twice, [k1 tbl, p1] twice, p4, k1 tbl, p1, k2tog, k6, yo, p5, yo, k6, SKP, p1, k1 tbl, p5, [k1 tbl, p1] twice, k1, p1, k1.

Row 24 [P1, k1] twice, [p1 tbl, k1] twice, k4, p1

tbl, k1, p7, p1 tbl, k5, p1 tbl, p7, k1, p1 tbl, k5, [p1 tbl, k1] twice, p1, k1, p1.

Row 25 P1, k1, p2, [k1 tbl, p1] twice, p4, k1 tbl, k2tog, k6, yo, k1 tbl, p5, k1 tbl, yo, k6, SKP, k1 tbl, p5, [k1 tbl, p1] twice, p1, k1, p1.

Row 26 K1, p1, k2, [p1 tbl, k1] twice, k4, p1 tbl, p7, p2 tbl, k5, p2 tbl, p7, p1 tbl, k5, [p1 tbl, k1] twice, k1, p1, k1.

Row 27 [K1, p1] twice, [k1 tbl, p1] twice, p4, k2tog, k6, yo, p1, k1 tbl, p5, k1 tbl, p1, yo, k6, SKP, p5, [k1 tbl, p1] twice, k1, p1, k1.

Row 28 [P1, k1] twice, [p1 tbl, k1] twice, k4, p7, p1 tbl, k1, p1 tbl, k5, p1 tbl, k1, p1 tbl, p7, k5, [p1 tbl, k1] twice, p1, k1, p1.

Row 29 P1, k1, p2, [k1 tbl, p1] twice, p3, k2tog, k6, yo, k1 tbl, p1, k1 tbl, p5, k1 tbl, p1, k1 tbl, yo, k6, SKP, p4, [k1 tbl, p1] twice, p1, k1, p1.

Row 30 K1, p1, k2, [p1 tbl, k1] twice, k3, p7, p2 tbl, k1, p1 tbl, k5, p1 tbl, k1, p2 tbl, p7, k4, [p1 tbl, k1] twice, k1, p1, k1.

Row 31 [K1, p1] twice, [k1 tbl, p1] twice, p2, k2tog, k6, yo, [p1, k1 tbl] twice, p5, [k1 tbl, p1] twice, yo, k6, SKP, p3, [k1 tbl, p1] twice, k1, p1, k1.

Row 32 [P1, k1] twice, [p1 tbl, k1] twice, k2, p7, [p1 tbl, k1] 3 times, k4, [p1 tbl, k1] twice, p1 tbl, p7, k3, [p1 tbl, k1] twice, p1, k1, p1.

Rep rows 1–32.

(worked over 32 sts and 26 rows)

Row 1 K11, p2, k2tog, m1, p2, m1, ssk, p2, k11.

Row 2 P11, k2, [p2, k2] twice, p11.

Row 3 K10, p2, k2tog, k1, m1, p2, m1, k1, ssk, p2, k10.

Row 4.P10, k2, [p3, k2] twice, p10.

Row 5 K9, p2, k2tog, k2, m1, p2, m1, k2, ssk, p2, k9.

Row 6 P9, k2, [p4, k2] twice, p9.

Row 7 K8, p2, k2tog, k3, m1, p2, m1, k3, ssk, p2, k8.

Row 8 P8, k2, [p5, k2] twice, p8.

Row 9 K7, p2, k2tog, k4, yo, p2, yo, k4, ssk, p2, k7.

Row 10 P7, k2, [p6, k2] twice, p7.

Row 11 K6, p2, k2tog, k4, yo, k1, p2, k1, yo, k4, ssk, p2, k6.

Row 12 P6, k2, [p7, k2] twice, p6.

Row 13 K5, p2, k2tog, k4, yo, k2, p2, k2, yo, k4, ssk, p2, k5.

Row 14 P5, k2, [p8, k2] twice, p5.

Row 15 K4, p2, k2tog, k4, yo, k3, p2, k3, yo, k4, ssk, p2, k4.

Row 16 P4, k2, [p9, k2] twice, p4.

Row 17 K3, p2, k2tog, k4, yo, k4, p2, k4, yo, k4, ssk, p2, k3.

Row 18 P3, k2, [p10, k2] twice, p3.

Row 19 K2, p2, k2tog, k4, yo, k5, p2, k5, yo, k4, ssk, p2, k2.

Row 20 P2, k2, [p11, k2] twice, p2.

Row 21 K1, p2, k2tog, k4, yo, k6, p2, k6, yo, k4, ssk, p2, k1.

Row 22 P1, k2, [p12, k2] twice, p1.

Row 23 P2, k2tog, k4, yo, k7, p2, k7, yo, k4, ssk, p2.

Row 24 K2, [p13, k2] twice.

Row 25 P2, [k13, p2] twice.

Row 26 K2, [p13, k2] twice.

100

101 seafoam pattern

(multiple of 10 sts plus 6)

Rows 1 and 2 Knit.

Row 3 (RS) K6, *yo, k1, [yo] twice, k1, [yo] 3 times, k1, [yo] twice, k1, yo, k6; rep from * to end.

Row 4 Knit, dropping all yo's off needle.

Rows 5 and 6 Knit.

Row 7 K1; *yo, k1, [yo] twice, k1, [yo] 3 times, k1, [yo] twice, k1, yo, k6; rep from *end k1.

Row 8 Rep row 4.

Rep rows 1–8.

102 purl shell stitch

(multiple of 6 sts plus 3)

Rows 1 and 2 Knit.

Row 3 (RS) K1, (k1, yo, k1) in next st, *k5 wrapping yarn twice for each st, (k1, yo, k1, yo, k1) in next st; rep from * to last 7 sts, k5 wrapping yarn twice for each (k1, yo, k1) in next st, k1.

Row 4 K4, *wyif sl 5 dropping extra wraps, then insert LH needle back into these 5 long sts and p5tog, k5; rep from *, end last rep k4.

Rows 5 and 6 Knit.

Row 7 K1, k3 wrapping yarn twice for each st, *(k1, yo, k1, yo, k1) in next st, k5 wrapping yarn twice for each st; rep from *, to last 5 sts, (k1, yo, k1, yo, k1), k3 wrapping yarn twice for each st, k1.

Row 8 K1, wyif sl 3 dropping extra wraps, then insert LH needle back into these 3 long sts and p3tog, *k5, wyif sl 5 dropping extra wraps, then insert LH needle back into these 5 long sts and p5tog; rep from *, end last rep wyif sl 3 dropping extra wraps, then insert LH needle back into these 3 long sts and p3tog, k1.

Rep rows 1–8.

lace

101

102

103 evergreen lace

(multiple of 14 sts plus 12)

Sl St (slip stitch)

Sl next st (sts) letting extra yo's fall.

CS (cluster stitch)

Insert RH needle (from behind) underneath the 5 long strands created by the dropped yo, then p1, k1 into these strands.

Row 1 (RS) K4 tbl, SKP, yo twice, *SKP, k4 tbl, k2, k4 tbl, SKP, yo twice; rep from *, end SKP, k4 tbl.

Row 2 P3, p2tog tbl, yo, *yo, sl st, p2tog tbl, p8, p2tog tbl, yo; rep from *, end yo, sl st, p2tog tbl, p3.

Row 3 K2, SKP, yo twice, *sl sts, SKP, k6, SKP, yo twice; rep from *, end sl sts, SKP, k2.

Row 4 P1, p2tog tbl, yo twice, *sl st, p2tog tbl, p4, p2tog tbl, yo twice; rep from *, end sl st, p2tog tbl, p1.

Row 5 SKP, yo twice, *sl st, SKP, k2, SKP, yo twice; rep from *, end sl st SKP.

Row 6 P1, yo 4 times, *CS, yo 4 times, p4, yo 4 times; rep from *, end CS, yo 4 times, p1.

Row 7 K1, k4 tbl, k2, *k4 tbl, SKP, yo twice, SKP, k4 tbl, k2; rep from *, end k4 tbl, k1.

Row 8 Yo twice, p2tog tbl, p3, *p5, p2tog tbl, yo twice, sl st, p2tog tbl, p3; rep from *, end p5, p2tog tbl, yo twice.

Row 9 Yo twice, sl st, SKP, k4, *k2, SKP, yo twice, sl st, SKP, k4; rep from *, end k2, SKP, yo twice, sl st.

Row 10 Yo twice, sl sts, p2tog tbl, p1, *p3, p2tog tbl, yo twice, sl st, p2tog tbl, p1; rep from *, end p3, p2tog tbl, yo twice, sl st.

Row 11 Yo twice, sl sts, SKP, k2, *SKP, yo twice, sl st, SKP, k2; rep from *, end SKP, yo twice, sl st.

Row 12 CS, yo 4 times, p1, *p3, yo 4 times, CS, yo 4 times, p1; rep from *, end p3, yo 4 times, CS.

Row 13 SK2P, k3 tbl, k2tog, yo twice, *SKP, k4 tbl, k2, k4 tbl, k2tog, yo twice; rep from *, end SKP, k3 tbl, sl 1-k2tog-psso.

Rep rows 2–13.

104 ripples and ridges

(multiple of 13 sts)

Rows 1, 2, 3 Knit.

Row 4 Purl.

Row 5 *K4, [yo, k1] 5 times, yo, k4; rep from * to end.

Row 6 Purl.

Row 7 *[K2tog] 3 times, k7, [ssk] 3 times; rep from * to end.

Row 8 Knit.

Rep rows 1-8.

104

105 scalloped shell

(multiple of 10 sts plus 1)

Double yo

Insert RH needle into next st wrapping yarn around needle twice, complete knit st.

Row 1 (RS) Knit.

Row 2 Purl.

Rows 3 and 4 Knit.

Row 5 *K1, [yo, k1] twice, [double yo] 5 times, [k1, yo] twice; rep from *, end k1.

Row 6 *K5, wyif sl 5 purlwise (dropping extra yo), k4; rep from *, end k1.

Row 7 *K5, wyib sl 5 purlwise, k4; rep from *, end k1.

Row 8 *P5, p5tog, p4; rep from *, end k1.

Rep rows 1–8.

106 scallop pattern

(multiple of 21 sts plus 3)

4-st wrap

P4, sl these sts to cn and hold away from needles, wrap yarn around the 4 sts counterclockwise 3 times, return sts to RH needle.

Rows 1 and 3 (WS) Knit.

Row 2 Purl.

Row 4 K1, *yo, k21; rep from *, end k2.

Row 5 P2, *p1, [k3, p1] 5 times, p1; rep from *, end p1.

Row 6 K1, *k1, yo, [k1, p3] 5 times, k1, yo; rep from *, end k2.

Row 7 P2, *p2, [k3, p1] 5 times, p2; rep from *, end p1.

Row 8 K1, *[k1, yo] twice, [SKP, p2] 5 times, [k1, yo] twice; rep from *, end k2.

Row 9 P2, *p4, [k2, p1] 5 times, p4; rep from *, end p1.

Row 10 K1, *[k1, yo] 4 times, [SKP, p1] 5 times, [k1, yo] 4 times; rep from *, end k2.

Row 11 P2, *p8, [k1, p1] 5 times, p8; rep from *, end p1.

Row 12 K1, *k8, SKP 5 times, k8; rep from *, end k2.

Row 13 P2, *p8, 4-st wrap, p9; rep from *, end p1.

Row 14 Knit.

Rep rows 1–14.

105

106

lace

(multiple of 22 sts plus 1)

Cluster Stitch

Sl given number of sts wyib, pass yarn to front, sl same sts back to LH needle, pass yarn to back, sl same sts again wyib, pass yarn to front, ready to purl next st.

Row 1 (RS) K1 *yo, [k1 tbl, p3] 5 times, k1 tbl, yo, k1; rep from * to end.

Row 2 P3, *[k3, p1] 4 times, k3, p5; rep from *, end last rep p3.

Row 3 K1 *yo, k1 tbl, yo, [k1 tbl, p3] 5 times, [k1 tbl, yo] twice, k1; rep from * to end.

Row 4 P5, *[k3, p1] 4 times, k3, p9; rep from *, end last rep p5.

Row 5 K1, *yo, k1 tbl, yo, ssk, yo, [k1 tbl, p2tog, p1] 5 times, k1 tbl, yo, k2tog, yo, k1 tbl, yo, k1; rep from * to end.

Row 6 P7, *[k2, p1] 4 times, k2, p13; rep from *, end last rep p7.

Row 7 K1, *k1 tbl, [yo, ssk] twice, yo, [k1 tbl, p2] 5 times, k1 tbl, yo, [k2tog, yo] twice, k1 tbl, k1; rep from * to end.

Row 8 P8, *[k2, p1] 4 times, k2, p15; rep from *, end last rep p8.

Row 9 K2, *[yo, k2tog] twice, yo, k1 tbl, yo, [k1 tbl, p2tog] 5 times, [k1 tbl, yo] twice, [ssk, yo] twice, k3; rep from *, end last rep k2.

Row 10 and 12 P10, *[k1, p1] 4 times, k1, p19; rep from *, end last rep p10.

Row 11 Ssk, *[yo, k2tog] 3 times, k1 tbl, yo, [k1 tbl, p1] 5 times, k1 tbl, yo, k1 tbl, [ssk, yo] 3 times, sl 1-k2tog-psso; rep from *, end last rep k2tog.

Row 13 K1, *[k2tog, yo] twice, k2tog, k1, k1 tbl, yo, [ssk] twice, sl 1-k2tog-psso, [k2tog] twice, yo, k1 tbl, k1, ssk, [yo, ssk] twice, k1; rep from * to end.

Row 14 Cluster 2, *p7, cluster 5, p7, cluster 3; rep from *, end last rep cluster 2.

Rep rows 1–14.

107

108 ostrich feather lace

(multiple of 16 sts plus 1)

Row 1 (RS) K1, *[yo, k1] twice, yo, ssk twice, sl 2sts knitwise-k1-psso, k2tog twice, [yo, k1] 3 times; rep from * to end.

Row 2 and all WS rows Purl.

Row 3 Knit.

Rows 5–16 Rep rows 1–4 three times.

Row 17 K2tog, *k2tog twice, [yo, k1]5 times, yo, ssk twice, sl 1-k2tog-psso; rep from *, end k2tog.

Row 19 Knit.

Rows 21–32 Rep rows 17–20 three times.

Rep rows 1–32.

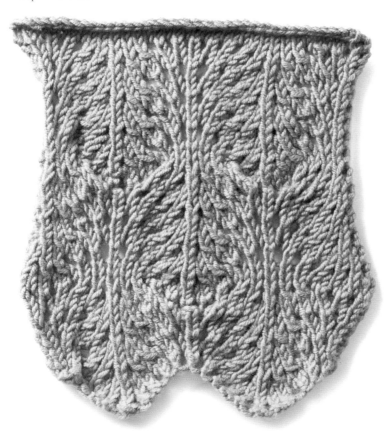

108

109 lace pattern

(multiple of 12 sts)

Row 1 (RS) *Yo, k2tog; rep from * to end.

Rows 2 and 4 Purl.

Row 3 Knit.

Row 5 *sl 1-k2 tog-psso, k4, yo, k1, yo, k4; rep from * to end.

Rows 6, 7 and 9 *P3tog, p4, yo, p1, yo, p4; rep from * to end.

Row 8 Rep row 5.

Row 10 *Yo, k2tog; rep from * to end.

Rows 11 and 13 Purl.

Row 12 Knit.

Row 14 Rep row 5.

Rows 15 and 16 Rep row 6.

Row 17 Rep row 5.

Row 18 Rep row 6.

Rep rows 1–18.

109

110 large eyelet diamonds

(worked over 27 sts)

SKP Slip 1, knit 1, pass slip st over

Row 1 (RS) K2, p23, k2.

Row 2 and all WS rows P2, k1, p21, k1, p2.

Row 3 K2, p1, k8, k2tog, yo, k1, yo, SKP, k8, p1, k2.

Row 5 K2, p1, k7, k2tog, yo, k3, yo, SKP, k7, p1, k2.

Row 7 K2, p1, k6, [k2tog, yo] twice, k1, [yo, SKP] twice, k6, p1, k2.

Row 9 K2, p1, k5, [k2tog, yo] twice, k3, [yo, SKP] twice, k5, p1, k2.

Row 11 K2, p1, k4, [k2tog, yo] twice, k5, [yo, SKP] twice, k4, p1, k2.

Row 13 K2, p1, k3, [k2tog, yo] twice, k7, [yo, SKP] twice, k3, p1, k2.

Row 15 K2, p1, k2, [k2tog, yo] twice, k9, [yo, SKP] twice, k2, p1, k2.

Row 17 K2, p1, k1, [k2tog, yo] twice, k11, [yo, SKP] twice, k1, p1, k2.

Row 19 K2, p1, k1, [yo, SKP] twice, k11, [k2tog, yo] twice, k1, p1, k2.

Row 21 K2, p1, k2, [yo, SKP] twice, k9, [k2tog, yo] twice, k2, p1, k2.

Row 23 K2, p1, k3, [yo, SKP] twice, k7, [k2tog, yo] twice, k3, p1, k2.

Row 25 K2, p1, k4, [yo, SKP] twice, k5, [k2tog, yo] twice, k4, p1, k2.

Row 27 K2, p1, k5, [yo, SKP] twice, k3, [k2tog, yo] twice, k5, p1, k2.

Row 29 K2, p1, k6, [yo, SKP] twice, k1, [k2tog, yo] twice, k6, p1, k2.

Row 31 K2, p1, k7, yo, SKP, yo, sl 1-k2tog-psso, yo, k2tog, yo, k7, p1, k2.

Row 33 K2, p1, k8, yo, SKP, k1, k2tog, yo, k8, p1, k2.

Rows 35 K2, p1, k9, yo, sl 1-k2tog-psso, yo, k9, p1, k2.

Row 36 Rep row 2.

Rep rows 3–36.

110

111 small eyelet diamonds

(worked over 17 sts)
Row 1 (RS) K2, yo, ssk, k9, k2tog, yo, k2.
Row 2 and all WS rows Purl.
Row 3 K3, yo, ssk, k7, k2tog, yo, k3.
Row 5 K4, yo, ssk, k5, k2tog, yo, k4.
Row 7 K5, yo, ssk, k3, k2tog, yo, k5.
Row 9 K6, yo, ssk, k1, k2tog, yo, k6.
Row 11 K6, sl next st to RH needle, sl next st to cn and hold in front of work, sl next st to another cn and hold to back of work, sl st from RH needle to LH needle, k2tog, yo, k st held to back of work, yo, sl st held to front of work to LH needle, ssk (center twist made over 5 sts), k6.
Row 13 K5, k2tog, yo, k3, yo, ssk, k5.
Row 15 K4, k2tog, yo, k5, yo, ssk, k4.
Row 17 K3, k2tog, yo, k7, yo, ssk, k3.
Row 19 K2, k2tog, yo, k9, yo, ssk, k2.
Row 20 Purl.
Rep rows 1–20.

112 eyelet zigzag

(multiple of 7 sts)
Row 1 (RS) *K2, k2tog, yo, k3; rep from * to end.
Row 2 and all WS rows Purl.
Row 3 *K1, k2tog, yo, k4; rep from * to end.
Row 5 Knit.
Row 7 *K3, yo, SKP, k2; rep from * to end.
Row 9 *K4, yo, SKP, k1; rep from * to end.
Row 11 Knit.
Row 12 Purl.
Rep rows 1–12.

113 mini diamond

(multiple of 8 sts)
Row 1 (RS) *K1, k2tog, yo, k1, yo, ssk, k2; rep from * to end.
Rows 2 and all WS rows Purl.
Row 3 *K2tog, yo, k3, yo, ssk, k1; rep from * to end.
Row 5 *Yo, k5, yo, [sl 1-k2tog-psso]; rep from * to end.
Row 7 *Yo, ssk, k3, k2tog, yo, k1; rep from * to end.
Row 9 *K1, yo, ssk, k1, k2tog, yo, k2; rep from * to end.
Row 11 *K2, yo, [sl 1-k2tog-psso], yo, k3; rep from * to end.
Row 12 Purl.
Rep rows 1–12.

114 crossing spikes

(multiple of 10 sts plus 2)
Row 1 (RS) K1, *SKP, k5, k2tog, yo, k1, yo; rep from *, end k1.
Row 2 and all WS rows Purl.
Row 3 K1, *yo, SKP, k3, k2tog, yo, k1, yo, SKP; rep from *, end k1.
Row 5 K1, *k1, yo, SKP, k1, k2tog, yo, k2, yo, SKP; rep from *, end k1.
Row 7 K1, *k2, yo, SKP, yo, k3, yo, SKP; rep from *, end k1.
Row 9 K1, *k1, k2tog, yo, k1, yo, SKP, k2, yo, SKP; rep from *, end k1.
Row 11 K1, *k2tog, yo, k1, [yo, SKP] twice, k1, yo, SKP; rep from *, end k1.
Row 13 K1, *yo, k2, [yo, SKP, k1] twice, k2tog; rep from *, end, k1.
Row 15 K1, *k1, [k2, yo, SKP] twice, yo; rep from *, end k1.
Row 17 K1, *SKP, k2, yo, SKP, k1, k2tog, yo, k1, yo; rep from *, end k1.
Row 19 K1, *yo, SKP, k1, yo, SKP, k2tog, yo, k3; rep from *, end k1.
Row 21 K1, *k1, yo, SKP, k1, k2tog, yo, k4; rep from *, end k1.
Row 23 K1, *k2, yo, SKP, yo, k5; rep from *, end k1.
Row 24 Purl.
Rep rows 1–24.

113

114

115 leaf pattern

(multiple of 12 sts)

Row 1 (RS) *K4, k3tog tbl, k4, yo, k1, yo; rep from * to end.

Row 2 and all WS rows Purl.

Row 3 *Yo, k3, k3tog tbl, k3, yo, k3; rep from * to end.

Row 5 *K1, yo, k2, k3tog tbl, k2, yo, k4; rep from * to end.

Row 7 *K2, yo, k1, k3tog tbl, k1, yo, k5; rep from * to end.

Row 9 *K3, yo, k3tog tbl, yo, k6; rep from * to end.

Row 11 *K3, yo, k1, yo, k4, k3tog, tbl, k1; rep from * to end.

Row 13 *K2, yo, k3, yo, k3, k3tog tbl, k1; rep from * to end.

Row 15 *K1, yo, k5, yo, k2, k3tog tbl, k1; rep from * to end.

Row 17 *Yo, k7, yo, k1, k3tog tbl, k1; rep from * to end.

Row 19 *K9, yo, k3tog tbl, yo; rep from * to end.

Row 20 Purl.

Rep rows 1–20.

116 ripple pattern

(multiple of 18 sts)

Row 1 (RS) *[K2tog] 3 times, [k1, yo] 6 times, [k2tog] 3 times; rep from * to end.

Rows 2 and 3 Knit.

Row 4 Purl.

Rep rows 1–4.

115

116

(multiple of 16 sts plus 2)

Row 1 (RS) K1, *Yo, ssk, k4, [yo, ssk] 3 times, k4; rep from *, end k1.

Row 2 and all WS rows K1, purl to last st, k1.

Row 3 K1, *k1, yo, ssk, k4, [yo, ssk] twice, k3, k2tog, yo; rep from *, end k1.

Row 5 K1, *k2, yo, ssk, k4, yo, ssk, k3, k2tog, yo, k1; rep from *, end k1.

Row 7 K1, *k3, yo, ssk, k7, k2tog, yo, k2; rep from *, end k1.

Row 9 K1, *k4, yo, ssk, k5, k2tog, yo, k3; rep from *, end k1.

Row 11 K1, *k5, yo, ssk, k3, k2tog, yo, k4; rep from *, end k1.

Row 13 K1, *k6, yo, ssk, k1, k2tog, yo, k5; rep from *, end k1.

Row 15 K1, *k7, yo, sl 1-k2tog-psso, yo, k6; rep from *, end k1.

Row 17 K1, *k8, yo, ssk, k6; rep from *, end k1.

Row 19 K1, *k6, k2tog, yo, k1, yo, ssk, k5; rep from *, end k1.

Row 21 K1, *k5, k2tog, yo, k3, yo, ssk, k4; rep from *, end k1.

Row 23 K1, *k4, k2tog, yo, k5, yo, ssk, k3; rep from *, end k1.

Row 25 K1, *k3, k2tog, yo, k7, yo, ssk, k2; rep from *, end k1.

Row 27 K1, *k2, k2tog, yo, k9, yo, ssk, k1; rep from *, end k1.

Row 29 K1, *k1, k2tog, yo, k5, yo, ssk, k4, yo, ssk; rep from *, end k1.

Row 31 K1, *sl 1-k2tog-psso, yo, k5, [yo, ssk] twice, k4, yo; rep from *, end k1.

Row 32 K1, purl across to last st, k1.

Rep rows 1–32.

118 eyelet diamond

(worked over 17 sts)

Row 1 (RS) K6, k2tog, yo, k1, yo, ssk, k6.

Row 2 and all WS rows Purl.

Row 3 K5, k2tog, yo, k3, yo, ssk, k5.

Row 5 K4, [k2tog, yo] twice, k1, [yo, ssk] twice, k4.

Row 7 K3, [k2tog, yo] twice, k3, [yo, ssk] twice, k3.

Row 9 K2, [k2tog, yo] 3 times, k1, [yo, ssk] 3 times, k2.

Row 11 K1, [k2tog,yo] 3 times, k3, [yo, ssk] 3 times, k1.

Row 13 [K2tog, yo] 3 times, k5, [yo, ssk] 3 times.

Row 15 K1, [yo, ssk] 3 times, k3, [k2tog, yo] 3 times, k1.

Row 17 K2, [yo, ssk] 3 times, k1, [k2tog, yo] 3 times, k2.

Row 19 K3, [yo, ssk] twice, yo, sl1-k2tog-psso, yo, [k2tog, yo] twice, k3.

Row 21 K4, [yo, ssk] twice, k1, [k2tog, yo] twice, k4.

Row 23 K5, yo, ssk, yo, sl1-k2tog-psso, yo, k2tog, yo, k5.

Row 25 K6, yo, ssk, k1, k2tog, yo, k6.

Row 27 K7, yo, sl 1-k2tog-psso, yo, k7.

Row 28 Purl.

Rep rows 1–28.

119 diamonds and spades

SKP Slip 1, knit 1, pass slip st over

SK2P Slip 1, knit 2 together, pass slip st over the knit 2 together. Two stitches been decreased.

(multiple of 26 sts plus 2)

Row 1 (RS) K1, *p4, k2tog, yo, p3, k2tog, k2, yo, p1, yo, k2, SKP, p3, yo, SKP, p3; rep from *, end k1.

Row 2 and all WS rows K the knit sts, p the purl sts and k the yo's.

Row 3 K1, *p3, k2tog, yo, p3, k2tog, k2, p1, [yo, p1] twice, k2, SKP, p3, yo, SKP, p2; rep from *, end k1.

Row 5 K1, *p2, k2tog, yo, p3, k2tog, k2, p2, yo, p1, yo, p2, k2, SKP, p3, yo, SKP, p1; rep from *, end k1.

Row 7 K1, *p1, k2tog, yo, p3, k2tog, k2, p3, yo, p1, yo, p3, k2, SKP, p3, yo, SKP; rep from * end k1.

Row 9 K1, k2tog, *yo, p3, k2tog, k2, p4, yo, p1, yo, p4, k2, SKP, p3, yo, sl 1-k2tog-psso; rep from *, end last rep SKP instead of SK2P.

Row 11 K1, *p4, k2tog, k2, p5, yo, p1, yo, p5, k2, SKP, p3; rep from *, end k1.

Row 13 K1, *p3, k2tog, k2, p4, yo, k2tog, yo, p1, yo, SKP, p4, k2, SKP, p2; rep from *, end k1.

Row 15 K1, *p2, k2tog, k2, p4, yo, k2tog, [p1, yo] twice, p1, SKP, yo, p4, k2, SKP, p1; rep from *, end k1.

Row 17 K1, *p1, k2tog, k2, p4, yo, k2tog, p2, yo, p1, yo, p2, SKP, yo, p4, k2, SKP; rep from *, end k1.

Row 19 K1, k2tog, *k2, p4, yo, k2tog, p3, yo, p1, yo, p3, SKP, yo, p4, k2, sl 1-k2tog-psso; rep from *, end last rep SKP instead of sl 1-k2tog-psso.

Row 21 K1, *p1, yo, k2, SKP, p3, yo, SKP, p7, k2tog, yo, p3, k2tog, k2, yo; rep from *, end k1.

Row 23 K1, *p1, yo, p1, k2, SKP, p3, yo, SKP, p5, k2tog, yo, p3, k2tog, k2, p1, yo; rep from *, end k1.

Row 25 K1, *p1, yo, p2, k2, SKP, p3, yo, SKP, p3, k2tog, yo, p3, k2tog, k2, p2, yo; rep from *, end k1.

Row 27 K1, *p1, yo, p3, k2, SKP, p3, yo, SKP, p1, k2tog, yo, p3, k2tog, k2, p3, yo; rep from *, end k1.

Row 29 K1, *p1, yo, p4, k2, SKP, p3, yo,sl 1-k2tog-psso, yo p3, k2tog, k2, p4, yo; rep from *, end k1.

Row 31 K1, *p1, yo, p5, k2, SKP, p7, k2tog, k2, p5, yo; rep from *, end k1.

Row 33 K1, *p1, yo, SKP, yo, p4, k2, SKP, p5, k2tog, k2, p4, yo, k2tog, yo; rep *, end k1.

Row 35 K1, *p1, yo, p1, SKP, yo, p4, k2, SKP, p3, k2tog, k2, p4, yo, k2tog, p1, yo; rep from *, end k1.

Row 37 K1, *p1, yo, p2, SKP, yo, p4, k2, SKP, p1, k2tog, k2, p4, yo, k2tog, p2, yo; rep from *, end k1.

Row 39 K1, *p1, yo, p3, SKP, yo, p4, k2, sl 1-k2tog-psso, k2, p4, yo, k2tog, p3, yo; rep from *, end k1.

Row 40 Rep row 2.

Rep rows 1–40.

120 eyelet diamond

(multiple of 24 sts plus 2)

Row 1 (RS) K1, *k11, k2tog, yo, k11; rep from *, end k1.

Row 2 and all WS rows Purl.

Row 3 K1, *k1, yo, SKP, k1, k2tog, yo, k4, k2tog, yo, k1, yo, SKP, k4, yo, SKP, k1, k2tog, yo; rep from *, end k1.

Row 5 K1, *k2, yo, sl 1-k2tog-psso, yo, k4, k2tog, yo, k3, yo, sl 1-k2tog-psso, k4, yo, SK2P, yo, k1; rep from *, end k1.

Row 7 K1, *k1, k2tog, yo, k5, k2tog, yo, k5, yo, SKP, k5, yo, SKP; rep from *, end k1.

Row 9 K1, k2tog, *yo, k5, k2tog, yo, k7, yo, SKP, k5, yo, sl 1-k2tog-psso; rep from *, end last rep SKP.

Row 11 K1, *k6, k2tog, yo, k9, yo, SKP, k5; rep from *, end k1.

Row 13 K1, *k5, k2tog, yo, k11, yo, SKP, k4; rep from *, end k1.

Row 15 K1, *k4, k2tog, yo, k5, yo, sl 1-k2tog-psso, yo, k5, yo, SKP, k3; rep from *, end k1.

Row 17 K1, *k3, k2tog, yo, k5, k2tog, yo, k1, yo, SKP, k5, yo, SKP, k2; rep from *, end k1.

Row 19 K1, *k2, k2tog, yo, k4, yo, sl 1-k2tog-psso, yo, k3, yo, sl 1-k2tog-psso, yo, k4, yo, SKP, k1; rep from *, end k1.

Row 21 K1, *k1, k2tog, yo, k4, SKP, yo, k1, yo, SKP, k1, k2tog, yo, k1, yo, k2tog, k4, yo, SKP; rep from *, end k1.

Row 23 K1, k2tog, *yo, k4, k2tog, yo, k3, yo, sl 1-k2tog-psso, yo, k3, yo, SKP, k4, yo, sl 1-k2tog-psso; rep from *, end last rep SKP.

Row 25 K1, *k1,yo, SKP, k4, yo, SKP, k1, k2tog, yo, k1, yo, SKP, k1, k2tog, yo, k4, k2tog, yo; rep from *, end k1.

Row 27 K1, *k2, yo, SKP, k4, yo, sl 1-k2tog-psso, yo, k3, yo, sl 1-k2tog-psso, yo, k4, k2tog, yo, k1; rep from *, end k1.

Row 29 K1, *k3, yo, SKP, k5, yo, SKP, k1, k2tog, yo, k5, k2tog, yo, k2; rep from *, end k1.

Row 31 K1, *k4, yo, SKP, k5, yo, sl 1-k2tog-psso, yo, k5, k2tog, yo, k3; rep from *, end k1.

Row 33 K1, *k5, yo, SKP, k11, k2tog, yo, k4; rep from *, end k1.

Row 35 K1, *k6, yo, SKP, k9, k2tog, yo, k5; rep from *, end k1.

Row 37 K1, SKP, *yo, k5, yo, SKP, k7, k2tog, yo, k5, yo, sl 1-k2tog-psso; rep from *, end last rep k2tog.

Row 39 K1, *k1, yo, SKP, k5, yo, SKP, [k5, k2tog, yo] twice; rep from *, end k1.

Row 41 K1, *k2, yo, sl 1-k2tog-psso, yo, k4, yo, SKP, k3, k2tog, yo, k4, yo, sl 1-k2tog-psso, yo, k1; rep from *, end k1.

Row 43 K1, *k1, k2tog, yo, k1, yo, k2tog, k4, yo, SKP, k1, k2tog, yo, k4, SKP, yo, k1, yo, SKP; rep from *, end k1.

Row 45 K1, SKP, *yo, k3, yo, SKP, k4, yo, sl 1-k2tog-psso, yo, k4, k2tog, yo, k3, yo, sl 1-k2tog-psso; rep *, end last rep SKP.

Rep rows 2–45.

120

121 pointelle diamond with cable corners

(worked over 39 sts)

4-st LC

Sl 2 st to cn and hold to *front*, k2, k2 from cn.

4-st RC

Sl 2 st to cn and hold to *back*, k2, k2 from cn.

Row 1 (RS) P1, k4, p1, k12, yo, sl 1-k2tog-psso, yo, k12, p1, k4, p1.

Rows 2, 4, 6, 8, 10, 12, 14 and 16 K1, p4, k1, p27, k1, p4, k1.

Row 3 P1, 4-st LC, p1, k10, yo, k2tog, k3, yo, SKP, k10, p1, 4-st RC, p1.

Row 5 P1, k4, p1, k9, [k2tog, yo] twice, k1, [yo, SKP] twice, k9, p1, k4, p1.

Row 7 P1, 4-st LC, p1, k8, [k2tog, yo] twice, k3, [yo, SKP] twice, k8, p1, 4-st RC, p1.

Row 9 P1, k4, p1, k7, [k2tog, yo] 3 times, k1, [yo, SKP] 3 times, k7, p1, k4, p1.

Row 11 P1, 4-st LC, p1, k6, [k2tog, yo] 3 times, k3, [yo, SKP] 3 times, k6, p1, 4-st RC, p1.

Row 13 P1, k4, p1, k5, [k2tog, yo] 4 times, k1, [yo, SKP] 4 times, k5, p1, k4, p1.

Row 15 P1, 4-st LC, p1, k4, [k2tog, yo] 4 times, k3, [yo, SKP] 4 times, k4, p1, 4-st RC, p1.

Row 17 P1, k4, p1, k3, [k2tog, yo] 4 times, k5, [yo, SKP] 4 times, k3, p1, k4, p1.

Rows 18, 20, 22, 24, 26, 28, 30, 32, 34, 36, 38 and 40 Purl.

Row 19 K8, [k2tog, yo] 4 times, k1, yo, SKP, k1, k2tog, yo, k1, [yo, SKP] 4 times, k8.

Row 21 K7, [k2tog, yo] 4 times, k3, yo, sl 1-k2tog-psso, yo, k3, [yo, SKP] 4 times, k7.

Row 23 K6, [k2tog, yo] 4 times, k11, [yo, SKP] 4 times, k6.

Row 25 K5, [k2tog, yo] 4 times, [k1, yo, SKP, k1, k2tog, yo] twice, k1, [yo, SKP] 4 times, k5.

Row 27 K4, [k2tog, yo] 4 times, [k3, yo, sl 1-k2tog-psso, yo] twice, k3, [yo, SKP] 4 times, k4.

Row 29 K3, [k2tog, yo] 4 times, k17, [yo, SKP] 4 times, k3.

Row 31 K5, [yo, SKP] 4 times, [k1, k2tog, yo, k1, yo, SKP] twice, k1, [k2tog, yo] 4 times, k5.

Row 33 K6, [yo, SKP] 3 times, [yo, sl 1-k2tog-psso, yo, k3] twice, yo, sl 1-k2tog-psso, yo, [k2tog, yo] 3 times, k6.

Row 35 K7, [yo, SKP] 4 times, k9, [k2tog, yo] 4 times, k7.

Row 37 K8, [yo, SKP] 4 times, k1, k2tog, yo, k1, yo, SKP, k1, [k2tog, yo] 4 times, k8.

Row 39 K9, [yo, SKP] 3 times, yo, sl 1-k2tog-psso, yo, k3, yo, sl 1-k2tog-psso, yo, [k2tog, yo] 3 times, k9.

Row 41 [P1, k4] twice, [yo, SKP] 4 times, k3, [k2tog, yo] 4 times, [k4, p1] twice.

Rows 42, 44, 46, 48, 50, 52, and 54 Rep row 2.

Row 43 P1, 4-st LC, p1, k5, [yo, SKP] 4 times, k1, [k2tog, yo] 4 times, k5, p1, 4-st RC, p1.

Row 45 P1, k4, p1, k6, [yo, SKP] 3 times, yo, sl 1-k2tog-psso, yo, [k2tog, yo] 3 times, k6, p1, k4, p1.

Row 47 P1, 4-st LC, p1, k7, [yo, SKP] 3 times, k1, [k2tog, yo] 3 times, k7, p1, 4-st RC, p1.

Row 49 P1, k4, p1, k8, [yo, SKP] twice, yo, sl 1-k2tog-psso, yo, [k2tog, yo] twice, k8, p1, k4, p1.

Row 51 P1, 4-st LC, p1, k9, [yo, SKP] twice, k1, [k2tog, yo] twice, k9, p1, 4-st RC, p1.

Row 53 P1, k4, p1, k10, yo, SKP, yo, sl 1-k2tog-psso, yo, k2tog, yo, k10, p1, k4, p1.

Row 55 P1, 4-st LC, p1, k11, yo, SKP, k1, k2tog, yo, k11, p1, 4-st RC, p1.

Row 56 Rep row 2.

Row 57 Rep row 1.

121

122 wings of desire lace panel

(worked over 19 sts)

Row 1 (RS) P2, SKP, k5, yo, k1, yo, k5, k2tog, p2.
Row 2 K2, p2tog, p5, yo, p1, yo, p5, p2tog tbl, k2.
Row 3 P2, SKP, k4, yo, k3, yo, k4, k2tog, p2.
Row 4 K2, p2tog, p4, yo, p3, yo, p4, p2tog tbl, k2.
Row 5 P2, SKP, k3, yo, k5, yo, k3, k2tog, p2.
Row 6 K2, p2tog, p3, yo, p5, yo, p3, p2tog tbl, k2.
Row 7 P2, SKP, k2, yo, k7, yo, k2, k2tog, p2.
Row 8 K2, p2tog, p2, yo, p7, yo, p2, p2tog tbl, k2.
Row 9 P2, SKP, k1, yo, k9, yo, k1, k2tog, p2.
Row 10 K2, p2tog, p1, yo, p9, yo, p1, p2tog tbl, k2.
Rep rows 1–10.

123 stag lace

(worked over of 23 sts)

Row 1 (RS) K8, k2tog, yo, k1, p1, k1, yo, ssk, k8.
Row 2 P7, p2tog tbl, p2, yo, k1, yo, p2, p2tog, p7.
Row 3 K6, k2tog, k1, yo, k2, p1, k2, yo, k1, ssk, k6.
Row 4 P5, p2tog tbl, p3, yo, p1, k1, p1, yo, p3, p2tog, p5.
Row 5 K4, k2tog, k2, yo, k3, p1, k3, yo, k2, ssk, k4.
Row 6 P3, p2tog tbl, p4, yo, p2, k1, p2, yo, p4, p2tog, p3.
Row 7 K2, k2tog, k3, yo, k4, p1, k4, yo, k3, ssk, k2.
Row 8 P1, p2tog tbl, p5, yo, p3, k1, p3, yo, p5, p2tog, p1.
Row 9 K2tog, k4, yo, k5, p1, k5, yo, k4, ssk.
Row 10 P11, k1, p11.
Row 11 K11, p1, k11.
Row 12 Rep row 10
Rep rows 1–12 .

124 fern lace

(multiple of 12 sts plus 3)

Row 1 (RS) K1, k2tog, k4, yo, *k1, yo, k4, sl 1-k2tog-psso, k4, yo; rep from *, end k1, yo, k4, SKP, k1.

Row 2 and all WS rows Purl.

Row 3 K1, k2tog, k3, yo, k1, *k2, yo, k3, sl 1-k2tog-psso, k3, yo, k1; rep from *, end k2, yo, k3, SKP, k1.

Row 5 K1, k2tog, k2, yo, k1, yo, *sl 1-k2tog-psso, yo, k1, yo, k2, sl 1-k2tog-psso, k2, yo, k1, yo; rep from *, end sl 1-k2tog-psso, yo, k1, yo, k2, SKP, k1.

Row 7 K1, k2tog, k1, yo, k2, yo, *sl 1-k2tog-psso, yo, k2, yo, k1, sl 1-k2tog-psso, k1, yo, k2, yo; rep from *, end sl 1-k2tog-psso, yo, k2, yo, k1, SKP, k1.

Row 9 K2, yo, SKP, K2tog, yo, k1, *k2, yo, SKP, k2tog, yo, k1, yo, SKP, k2tog, yo, k1, from *, end k2, yo, SKP, k2tog, yo, k2.

Row 10 Purl.

Rep rows 1–10.

125 ravelling leaves

(multiple of 18 sts plus 2)

Row 1 and all WS rows Purl.

Row 2 RS P2, *k9, yo, k1, yo, k3, [sl 1-k2tog-psso], p2; rep from * to end.

Row 4 P2, *k10, yo, k1, yo, k2, sl 1-k2tog-psso, p2; rep from * to end.

Row 6 P2, *k3tog, k4, yo, k1, yo, k3, [yo, k1] twice, sl-1-k2tog-psso, p2; rep from * to end.

Row 8 P2, *k3tog, k3, yo, k1, yo, k9, p2; rep from * to end.

Row 10 P2, *k3tog, k2, yo, k1, yo, k10, p2; rep from * to end.

Row 12 P2, *k3tog, [k1, yo] twice, k3, yo, k1, yo, k4, sl-1-k2tog-psso, p2; rep from * to end.

Rep rows 1–12.

126 feather lace

(multiple of 16 sts plus 1)

Row 1 (RS) *P1, k5, [yo, k1] 4 times, k2; rep from *, end p1.

Row 2 and all WS rows *K1, p15; rep from *, end k1.

Row 3 *P1, k3, k2tog twice, [yo, k1] 3 times, yo, ssk twice, k1; rep from *, end p1.

Row 5 *P1, k2, k2tog twice, [yo, k1] twice, k1, [k1, yo] twice, ssk twice; rep from *, end p1.

Row 7 *P1, k1, k2tog twice, [yo, k1] 3 times, yo, ssk twice, k3; rep from *, end p1.

Row 9 *P1, k2tog twice, [yo, k1] twice, k1, [k1, yo] twice, ssk twice, k2; rep from *, end p1.

Row 10 Rep row 2.

Rep rows 3–10.

127 falling leaves pattern

(multiple of 15 sts plus 1)

Row 1 *K1, yo, k1, k2tog tbl, p1, k2tog, k1, yo, p1, k2tog tbl, p1, k2tog, yo, k1, yo; rep from * end k1.

Row 2 P1, *p4, k1, p1, k1, p3, k1, p4; rep from * to end.

Row 3 *K1, yo, k1, k2tog tbl, p1, k2tog, k1, p1, sl 1-k2tog-psso, yo, k3, yo; rep from *, end k1.

Row 4 P1, *p6, k1, p2, k1, p4; rep from * to end.

Row 5 *[K1, yo] twice, k2tog tbl, p1, [k2tog] twice, yo, k5, yo; rep from *, end k1.

Row 6 P1, *p7, k1, p1, k1, p5; rep from * to end.

Row 7 *K1, yo, k3, yo, sl 1-k2tog-psso, p1, yo, k1, k2tog tbl, p1, k2tog, k1, yo; rep from *, end k1.

Row 8 P1, *[p3, k1] twice, p7; rep from * to end.

Row 9 *K1, yo, k5, yo, k2tog tbl, k1, k2tog tbl, p1, k2tog, k1, yo; rep from *, end k1.

Row 10 P1, *p3, k1, p2, k1, p8; rep from * to end.

Rep rows 1–10.

126

127

128 eternal flame

(multiple of 8 sts plus 2)

Row 1 (RS) K1* yo, SKP, k6; rep from *, end k1.

Row 2 and all WS rows K1, purl to last st, k1.

Rows 3, 5, 7 and 9 K1, * k1, yo, k2, sl 1-k2tog-psso, k2, yo; rep from * , end k1.

Row 11 K1, *k4, yo, SKP, k2; rep from *, end k1.

Rows 13, 15, 17 and 19 K1, k2tog,*k2, yo, k1, yo, k2, sl 1-k2tog-psso; rep from * to last 7 sts, end k2, [yo, k1] twice, SKP, k1.

Row 20 K1, purl to last st, k1.

Rep rows 1–20.

129 pointelle leaf pattern

(multiple of 8 sts plus 4)

Note Sts are inc on all RS rows and dec back to original number on WS rows.

Row 1 (RS) K2, *yo, k1 tbl, yo, ssk, k5; rep from *, end k2.

Row 2 P6, *p2tog tbl, p7; rep from *, end last rep p5.

Row 3 K2, *yo, k1 tbl, yo, k2, ssk, k3; rep from *, end k2.

Row 4 P4, *p2tog tbl, p7; rep from * to end.

Row 5 K2, *k1 tbl, yo, k4, ssk, k1, yo; rep from *, end k2.

Row 6 P3, *p2tog tbl, p7; rep from *, end p1.

Row 7 K2, *k5, k2tog, yo, k1 tbl, yo; rep from *, end k2.

Row 8 P5, *p2tog, p7; rep from *, end last rep p6.

Row 9 K2, *k3, k2tog, k2, yo, k1 tbl, yo; rep from *, end k2.

Row 10 *P7, p2tog, rep from *, end p4.

Row 11 K2, *yo, k1, k2tog, k4, yo, k1 tbl; rep from *, end k2.

Row 12 P1, *p7, p2tog; rep from *, end p3.

Rep rows 1–12.

128

129

130 diamond trellis

(multiple of 12 sts plus 5)

Row 1 (RS) K1, yo, sl 1-k2tog-psso, [yo, k2tog] twice, yo, *k1, [yo, SKP] twice, yo, sl 1-k2tog-psso, [yo, k2tog] twice, yo; rep from *, to last 9 sts end k1, [yo, SKP] twice, yo, sl 1-k2tog-psso, yo, k1.

Row 2 and all WS rows Purl.

Row 3 K3, [k2tog, yo] twice, k1, *k2, [yo, SKP] twice, k1, [k2tog, yo] twice, k1; rep from * to last 9 sts, end k2, [yo, SKP] twice, k3.

Row 5 Rep row 1.

Row 7 Rep row 3.

Row 9 Rep row 1.

Row 11 K2tog, yo, k1, [yo, SKP] twice, yo, *sl 1-k2tog-psso, [yo, k2tog] twice, yo, k1, [yo, SKP] twice, yo; rep from * last 10 sts, end sl 1-k2tog-psso, [yo, k2tog] twice, yo, k1, yo, SKP.

Row 13 K4, [yo, SKP] twice, *k1, [k2tog, yo] twice, k3; [yo, SKP] twice; rep from *, end k1, [k2tog, yo] twice, k4.

Row 15 Rep row 11.

Row 17 Rep row 13.

Row 19 Rep row 11.

Row 20 Purl.

Rep rows 1–20.

(worked over 17 sts)

Cluster 3

Wyib sl 3, bring yarn to front, sl same 3 sts back to LH needle, bring yarn to back, k3.

Double Inc.

[K1 tbl, k1] in one st, insert LH needle behind vertical strand between the 2 sts just made and k1 tbl in this strand.

Dec 4

sl 1, k3tog, psso.

Row 1 (RS) K7, cluster 3, k7.

Row 2 and all WS rows Purl.

Row 3 K5, k3tog, yo, double inc, yo, k3tog tbl, k5.

Row 5 K3, k3tog, yo, k2tog, yo, double inc, yo, ssk, yo, k3tog tbl, k3.

Row 7 K2, [k2tog, yo] 3 times, k1 tbl, [yo, ssk] 3 times, k2.

Row 9 K3, [yo, k2tog] twice, yo, sl 1-k2tog-psso, [yo, ssk] twice, yo, k3.

Row 11 K2, [ssk, yo] 3 times, k1 tbl, [yo, k2tog] 3 times, k2.

Row 13 K3, inc 1, yo, ssk, yo, dec 4, yo, k2tog, yo, inc 1, k3.

Row 15 K5, in1, yo, dec 4, yo, inc 1, k5.

Row 17 K7, cluster 3, k7.

Row 18 Purl.

131

132 thistle lace

(multiple of 10 sts plus 1)

Sl2b-p1k1-p2sso sl 2 sts tog purlwise tbl onto RH needle, P1(k1), pass bothe sl sts tog over the p1 (k1) st.

Rows 1, 2, 3, 4 and 5 Knit.

Row 6 (WS) P1, *yo, p3, sl2b-p1-p2sso, p3, yo, p1; rep from * to end.

Row 7 K2, *yo, k2, sl2b-k1-p2sso, k2, yo, k3; rep from *, end last rep k2.

Row 8 P3, *yo, p1, sl2b-p1-p2sso, p1, yo, p5; rep from *, end last rep p3.

Row 9 K4, *yo, sl2b-k1-p2sso, yo, k7; rep from * , end last rep k4.

Row 10 P2, *k2, p3; rep from *, end last rep p2.

Row 11 K1, *yo, SKP, p1, yo, sl2b-k1-p2sso, yo, p1, k2tog, yo, k1; rep from * to end.

Row 12 P3, *k1, p3, k1, p5; rep from *, end last rep p3.

Row 13 K2, *yo, SKP, yo, sl2b-k1-p2sso, yo, k2tog, yo, k3; rep from *, end last rep k2.

Row 14 P2, *k1, p5, k1, p3; rep from *, end last rep p2.

Row 15 K2, *p1, k1, yo, sl2b-k1-p2sso, yo, k1, p1, k3,; rep from *, end last rep k2.

Row 16 Rep row 14.

Rep rows 1–16.

132

133 pointelle

(multiple of 14 sts plus 5)

Row 1 (RS) *K5, yo, SKP , k2, p1, k2, k2tog, yo; rep from *, end k5.

Rows 2 and 4 P9, *k1, p13; rep from * end k1, p9.

Row 3 K6, *yo, SKP, k1, p1, k1, k2tog, yo, k7; rep from *, end last rep k6.

Row 5 K7, *yo, SKP, p1, k2tog, yo, k9, rep from *, end last rep k7.

Row 6 rep as row 2.

Rep rows 1–6.

133

134 chevron eyelet

(multiple of 11 sts)

Row 1 (RS) *K3, k2tog, yo, k1, yo, k2tog tbl, k3; rep from * to end.

Row 2 and all WS rows Purl.

Row 3 *K2, k2tog, yo, k3, yo, k2tog tbl, k2; rep from * to end.

Row 5 *K1, k2tog, yo, k5, yo, k2tog tbl, k1; rep from * to end.

Row 7 *K2tog, yo, k7, yo, k2tog tbl; rep from * to end.

Row 8 Purl.

Rep rows 1–8.

135 foliage lace

(multiple of 20 sts)

Row 1 (RS) *K5, p2tog, k2, yo, k5, yo, k2, p2tog, k2; rep from * to end.

Row 2 and all WS rows Purl.

Row 3 *K4, p2tog, k2, yo, k1, yo, k2, p2tog, k7; rep from * to end.

Row 5 *K3, p2tog, k2, yo, k3, yo, k2, p2tog, k6; rep from * to end.

Row 7 *K2, p2tog, k2, yo, k5, yo, k2, p2tog, k5; rep from * to end.

Row 9 *K7, p2tog, k2, yo, k1, yo, k2, p2tog, k4; rep from * to end.

Row 11 *K6, p2tog, k2, yo, k3, yo, k2, p2tog, k3; rep from * to end.

Row 12 Purl.

Rep rows 1–12.

lace

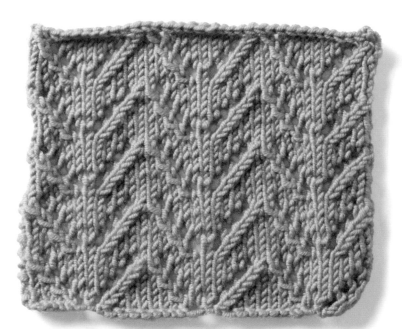

134

135

136 pointelle

(worked over 17 sts)

Row 1 (RS) SKP, yo, k2, k2tog, yo, k1, yo, sl 1-k2tog-psso, yo, k1, yo, SKP, k2, yo, k2tog.

Row 2 and all WS rows Purl.

Row 3 SKP, k3, yo, k2tog, yo, k3, yo, SKP, yo, k3, k2tog.

Row 5 SKP, [k2, yo] twice, k2tog, k1, SKP, [yo, k2] twice, k2tog.

Row 7 SKP, k1, yo, k3, yo, k2tog, k1, SKP, yo, k3, yo, k1, k2tog.

Row 8 Purl.

Rep rows 1–8.

137 fern lace

(multiple of 10 sts plus 4)

Row 1 (RS) K2, k2tog, k1, *k2, yo, k1, yo, k3, sl 2 knitwise k1 p2sso, k1; rep from *, end last rep SKP, k1.

Row 2 and all WS rows Purl.

Row 3 K1, k2tog, k2, *[k1, yo] twice, k3, sl 2 knitwise-k1-psso, k2; rep from *, end last rep SKP, k2.

Row 5 K2tog, k3, *yo, k1, yo, k3, sl 2 knitwise, k1, p2sso, k3; rep from *, end last rep SKP, k3.

Row 7 Rep row 3.

Row 9 Rep row 1.

Row 11 K3, k2tog, *k3, yo, k1, yo, k3, sl 2 knitwise-k1-psso, k1, p2sso; rep from *, end last rep SKP.

Row 12 Purl.

Rep rows 1–12.

136

137

138 lace pattern

(multiple of 12 sts plus 3)

Row 1 (RS) K1, k2tog, k4, yo, *k1, yo, k4, sl 2 knitwise-k1-p2sso, k4, yo; rep from *, end last rep SKP, k1.

Row 2 and all WS rows Purl.

Row 3 K1, k2tog, k3, yo, k1, *k2, yo, k3, sl 2 knitwise-k1- p2sso, k3, yo, k1; rep from *, end last rep SKP, k1.

Row 5 K1, k2tog, k2, yo, k2, *yo, SKP, k1, yo, k2, sl 2 knitwisc-k1- p2sso, k2, yo, k2; rep from *, last rep SKP, k1.

Row 7 K1, k2tog, [k1, yo] twice, SKP, *k1, k2tog, [yo, k1] twice, sl 2 knitwise-k1-p2sso, [k1, yo] twice, SKP; rep from *, end last rep SKP, k1.

Row 9 K1, k2tog, yo, k3, yo, *k3tog, yo, k3, yo, sl 2 knitwise-k1-p2sso, yo, k3, yo; rep from last rep SKP, k1.

Row 10 Purl.

Rep rows 1–10.

139 sunrise, sunset

(multiple of 20 sts plus 1)

Row 1 (RS) *P5, k2tog, k3, yo, p1, yo, k3, SKP, p4; rep from *, end p1.

Row 2 and all WS rows Purl.

Row 3 *P4, k2tog, k3, yo, p3, yo, k3, SKP, p3; rep from *, end p1.

Row 5 *P3, k2tog, k3, yo, p5, yo, k3, SKP, p2; rep from *, end p1.

Row 7 *P2, k2tog, k3, yo, p7, yo, k3, SKP, p1; rep from *, end p1.

Row 9 *P1, k2tog, k3, yo, p9, yo, k3, SKP; rep from *, end p1.

Row 10 Purl.

Rep rows 1–10.

138

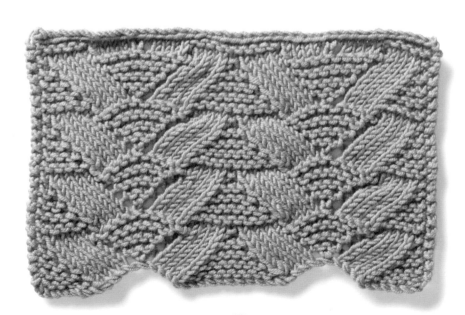

139

140 eyelet tulips

(multiple of 18 sts plus 1)

Row 1 (RS) K1, *yo, SKP, p3, yo, SKP, k3, k2tog, yo, p3, k2tog, yo, k1; rep from * to end.

Row 2 *P3, k3, p7, k3, p2; rep from *, end p1.

Row 3 K1, *yo, k1, SKP, p3, yo, SKP, k1, k2tog, yo, p3, k2tog, k1, yo, k1; rep from * to end.

Row 4 *P4, k3, p5, k3, p3; rep from *, end p1.

Row 5 K1, *yo, k2, SKP, p3, yo, sl 1-k2tog-psso, yo, p3, k2tog, k2, yo, k1; rep from * to end.

Row 6 *P5, k3, p3, k3, p4; rep from *, end p1.

Row 7 K1, *yo, k3, SKP, p7, k2tog, k3, yo, k1; rep from * to end.

Row 8 *P6, k7, p5; rep from *, end p1.

Row 9 K1, *yo, k4, SKP, p5, k2tog, k4, yo, k1; rep from * to end.

Row 10 *P7, k5, p6; rep from *, end p1.

Row 11 K1, *yo, k5, SKP, p3, k2tog, k5, yo, k1; rep from * to end.

Row 12 *P8, k3, p7; rep from *, end p1.

Row 13 K1, *yo, k6, SKP, p1, k2tog, k6, yo, k1; rep from * to end.

Rows 14 and 16 *P9, k1, p8; rep from *, end p1.

Row 15 K1, *yo, k2, k2tog, yo, SKP, k2, p1, k2, k2tog, yo, SKP, k2, yo, k1; rep from * to end.

Row 17 K1, *k2, k2tog, yo, p1, yo, SKP, k1, p1, k1, k2tog, yo, p1, yo, SKP, k3; rep from * to end.

Row 18 *P5, [k1, p3] twice, k1, p4; rep from *, end p1.

Row 19 K1, *k1, k2tog, yo, p3, k2tog, yo, k1, yo, SKP, p3, yo, SKP, k2; rep from * to end.

Row 20 *P4, k3, p5, k3, p3; rep from *, end p1.

Row 21 K1, *k2tog, yo, p3, k2tog, [k1, yo] twice, k1, SKP, p3, yo, SKP, k1; rep from * to end.

Row 22 *P3, k3, p7, k3, p2; rep from *, end p1.

Row 23 K2tog, *yo, p3, k2tog, k2, yo, k1, yo, k2, SKP, p3, yo, sl 1-k2tog-psso; rep from *, end last rep SKP.

Row 24 *P2, k3, p9, k3, p1; rep from *, end p1.

Row 25 P1, *p3, k2tog, k3, yo, k1, yo, k3, SKP, p4; rep from * to end.

Row 26 *K4, p11, k3; rep from *, end k1.

Row 27 P1, *p2, k2tog, k4, yo, k1, yo, k4, SKP, p3; rep from * to end.

Row 28 *K3, p13, k2; rep from *, end k1.

Row 29 P1, *p1, k2tog, k5, yo, k1, yo, k5, SKP, p2; rep from * to end.

Row 30 *K2, p15, k1; rep from *, end k1.

Row 31 P1, *k2tog, k6, yo, k1, yo, k6, SKP, p1; rep from * to end.

Rows 32 and 34 *K1, p17; rep from *, end k1.

Row 33 P1, *k2, k2tog, yo, SKP, k2, yo, k1, yo, k2, k2tog, yo, SKP, k2, p1; rep from * to end.

Row 35 P1, *k1, k2tog, yo, p1, yo, SKP, k5, k2tog, yo, p1, yo, SKP, k1, p1; rep from * to end.

Row 36 *K1, p3, k1, p9, k1, p3; rep from *, end k1.

Rep rows 1–36.

141 a coat of arms lace

(multiple of 18 sts plus 1)

Row 1 (RS) *K1, yo, k5, k2tog, yo, SK2P, yo, sl1-k2tog-psso, k5, yo; rep from *, end k1.

Row 2 and all WS rows Purl.

Row 3 *[K1, yo] twice, SKP, k2, k2tog, yo, sl1-k2tog-psso, yo, SKP, k2, k2tog, yo, k1, yo; rep from *, end k1.

Row 5 *K1, yo, k3, yo, SKP, k2tog, yo, sl1-k2tog-pss, yo, SKP, k2tog, yo, k3, yo; rep from *, end k1.

Row 7 *K1, yo, k5, yo, SKP, sl1-k2tog-pss, k2tog, yo, k5, yo; rep from *, end k1.

Row 8 Purl.

Rep rows 1–8 for lace pat.

142 trellis pattern

(multiple of 15 sts plus 4)

Row 1 RS K4, *[yo, ssk] twice, yo, sl 2 knitwise-k1-p2sso, [yo, k2tog] twice, yo, k1, p2, k1; rep from * to last 15 sts, [yo, ssk] twice, yo, sl 2 knitwise-k1-p2sso, [yo, k2tog] twice, yo, k4.

Rows 2 and 4 K3, *p13, k2; rep from * to last 16 sts, p13, k3.

Row 3 K3, *[yo, ssk] 3 times, k1, [k2tog, yo] 3 times, p2; rep from * to last 16 sts, [yo, ssk] 3 times, k1, [k2tog, yo] 3 times, k3.

Rep rows 1–4.

lace

141

142

143 arrowhead lace

(multiple of 10 sts plus 1)
Row 1 (WS) Purl.
Row 2 K1, *[yo, ssk twice, k1, [k2tog, yo] twice, k1; rep from * to end.
Row 3 Purl.
Row 4 K2, *yo, ssk, yo, sl 2 knitwise-k1-p2sso, yo, k2tog, yo, k3; rep from *, end last rep k2.
Rep rows 1–4.

144 chevron lace

(multiple of 8 sts plus 1)
s2pp
Sl 2 sts knitwise, one at a time, to RH needle and put them back on LH needle, then sl 2 sts tog as if to p2tog tbl, p next st, pass sl sts over p st and off needle.
Row 1 (RS) K1, *ssk, [k1, yo] twice, k1, k2tog, k1; rep from * to end.
Row 2 *P1, p2tog, [p1, yo] twice, p1, p2tog tbl; rep from *, end p1.
Row 3 K1, *yo, ssk, k3, k2tog, yo, k1; rep from * to end.
Row 4 *P2, yo, p2tog, p1, p2tog tbl, yo, p1; rep from *, end p1.
Row 5 K3, yo, sl 2 knitwise-k1-p2sso, yo, k3, *k2, yo, sl 2 knitwise-k1-p2sso, yo, k3; rep from * to end.
Row 6 Rep row 2.
Row 7 Rep row 1.
Row 8 *P1, yo, p2tog, p3, p2tog tbl, yo; rep from *, end p1.
Row 9 K2, yo, ssk, k1, k2tog, yo, k2, *k1, yo, ssk, k1, k2tog, yo, k2; rep from * to end.
Row 10 *P3, yo, s2pp, yo, p2; rep from *, end p1.
Rep rows 1–10.

145 eyelet hearts

(multiple of 12 sts plus 3)

SK4P

Sl next 4 sts knitwise, one at a time, insert LH needle into fronts of these sts and k them tog.

Row 1 (RS) K2, *yo, k2tog, k3, yo, k1, yo, k3, SKP, yo, k1; rep from *, end k1.

Row 2 and all WS rows Purl.

Row 3 K2, *k1, yo, k4tog, yo, k3, yo, SK4P, yo, k2; rep from *, end last k1.

Row 5 K2, *k1, k2tog, yo, k5, yo, SKP, k2; rep from *, end k1.

Row 7 K2, *k2tog, yo, k7, yo, SKP, k1; rep from *, end k1.

Row 9 K1, k2tog, *yo, k9, yo, sl 1-k2tog-psso; rep from *, end rep SKP, k1.

Row 10 Purl.

Rep rows 1–10.

146 subway lace

(multiple of 10 sts plus 4)

Row 1 and all WS rows Purl.

Row 2 K4, *yo, SKP, k1, [k2tog, yo] twice, k3; rep from * to end.

Row 4 *K3, [yo, SKP] twice, k1, k2tog, yo; rep from *, end k4.

Row 6 K2, *[yo, SKP] 3 times, k4; rep from *, end yo, SKP.

Row 8 K1, *[yo, SKP] 4 times, k2; rep from *, end yo, SKP, k1.

Row 10 Rep row 6.

Row 12 Rep row 4.

Row 14 Rep row 2.

Row 16 K2tog, yo, *k4, [k2tog, yo] 3 times; rep from *, end k2.

Row 18 K1, k2tog, yo, *k2, [k2tog, yo] 4 times; rep from *, end k1.

Row 20 Rep row 16.

Rep rows 1–20 for pat.

(multiple of 22 sts plus 1)

Row 1 and all WS rows Purl.

Row 2 Ssk, *[yo, ssk] twice, k3, [k2tog, yo] twice, sl 2 sts knitwise-k1-p2sso, yo, ssk, yo, [k1, yo, k1, yo, k1, yo, k1] in next st making 7 sts from 1; yo, k2tog, yo, sl 2 sts knitwise-k1-p2sso; rep from *, end last rep k2tog.

Row 4 Ssk, *[yo, ssk] twice, k1, [k2tog, yo] twice, sl 2 sts knitwise-k1-p2sso, yo, ssk, yo, k1, p5, k1, yo, k2tog, yo, sl 2 sts knitwise-k1-p2sso; rep from *, end last rep k2tog.

Row 6 Ssk, *yo, ssk, yo, sl 2 sts knitwise-k1-p2sso, yo, k2tog, yo, sl 2 sts knitwise-k1-p2sso, yo, ssk, yo, k1, p5, k1, yo, k2tog, yo, sl 2 sts knitwise-k1-p2sso; rep from *, end last rep k2tog.

Row 8 Ssk, *yo, ssk, yo, [k1, yo, k1, yo, k1, yo, k1] in next st, yo, k2tog, yo, sl 2 sts knitwise- k1-p2sso, [yo, ssk] twice, k3, [k2tog, yo] twice, sl 2 sts knitwise-k1-p2sso; rep from * end last rep k2tog.

Row 10 Ssk, *yo, ssk, yo, k1, p5, k1, yo, k2tog, yo, sl 2 sts knitwise-k1-p2sso,[yo, ssk] twice, k1, [k2tog, yo] twice, sl 2 sts knitwise-k1-p2sso; rep from *, end last rep k2tog.

Row 12 Ssk, *yo, ssk, yo, k1, p5, k1, yo, k2tog, yo, sl 2 sts knitwise-k1-p2sso, yo, ssk, yo, sl 2 sts knitwise-k1-p2sso, yo, k2tog, yo, sl 2 sts knitwise-k1-p2sso; rep from *, end last rep k2tog.

Rep rows 1–12.

147

148 eyelet pattern

(multiple of 6 sts plus 1)

Row 1 (RS) K1, *k2tog, yo, k1, yo, SKP, k1; rep from * to end.

Row 2 and all WS rows Purl.

Row 3 K1, *k1, yo, sl 2tog knitwise-k1-psso, yo, k2; rep from * to end.

Row 5 K1, *SKP, yo, k1, yo, k2tog, k1; rep from * to end.

Row 7 K1, yo, SKP, *k1, k2tog, yo, k1, yo, SKP; rep from *, end k1, k2tog, yo, k1.

Row 9 K2tog, yo, k1, *k2, yo, sl 2tog knitwise-k1-psso, yo, k1; rep from *, end k2, yo, SKP.

Row 11 K1, yo, k2tog, *k1, SKP, yo, k1, yo, k2tog; rep from *, end k1, SKP, yo, k1.

Row 12 Purl.

Rep rows 1–12.

149 eyelet posies

(multiple of 13 sts plus 2)

MB (make bobble)

[K1, k1 tbl] twice, k1] in one st—5 sts, turn, p5, turn, k5, turn, p2tog, p1, p2tog, turn, sl 1-k2tog-psso

Row 1 (RS) K1, *p4, k5, p4; rep from *, end k1.

Row 2 and all WS rows K the knit sts, p the purl sts and p yo sts.

Row 3 K1, *p3, k2tog, [k1, yo] twice, k1, ssk, p3; rep from *, end k1.

Row 5 K1, *p2, k2tog, k1, yo, k3, yo, k1, ssk, p2; rep from *, end k1.

Row 7 K1, *p1, k2tog, k1, yo, k5, yo, k1, ssk, p1; rep from *, end k1.

Row 9 K1, *k2tog, k1, yo, k3, MB, k3, yo, k1, ssk; rep from *, end k1.

Row 10 Rep row 2.

Rep rows 1–10.

lace

150 eyelet artichokes

(multiple of 18 sts plus 1)

Preparation Row 1 (RS) *K1, p2, k2, p4, k1, p4, k2, p2; rep from *, end k1.

Row 2 and all WS rows K the knit sts and p the purl sts, p the yo sts.

Row 3 *K1, yo, p2, k2, p3, k3tog, p3, k2, p2, yo; rep from *, end k1.

Row 5 *K1, yo, k1, p2, k2, p2, k3tog, p2, k2, p2, k1, yo; rep from *, end k1.

Row 7 *K1, yo, p1, k2, p2, k1, p1, k3tog, p1, k1, p2, k2, p1, yo; rep from *, end k1.

Row 9 *K1, yo, p2, k2, p2, k1, k3tog, k1, p2, k2, p2, yo; rep from *, end k1.

Row 11 *K1, yo, p3, k2, p2, k3tog, p2, k2, p3, yo; rep from *, end k1.

Row 13 K2tog, *p3, k2, p2, yo, k1, yo, p2, k2, p3, k3tog; rep from *, end last rep SKP instead of k3tog.

Row 15 K2tog, *p2, k2, p2, [k1, yo] twice, k1, p2, k2, p2, k3tog; rep from *, end last rep SKP instead of k3tog.

Row 17 K2tog, *p1, k1, p2, k2, p1, yo, k1, yo, p1, k2, p2, k1, p1, k3tog; rep from *, end last rep SKP instead of k3tog.

Row 19 K2tog, *k1, p2, k2, p2, yo, k1, yo, p2, k2, p2, k1, k3tog tbl; rep from *, end last rep SKP instead of k3tog.

Row 21 K2tog, *p2, k2, p3, yo, k1, yo, p3, k2, p2, k3tog tbl; rep from *, end lst rep SKP instead of k3tog.

Row 22 Rep row 2.

Rep rows 3–22.

151 rose trellis

(multiple of 18 sts plus 5)

MB (make bobble)

[K, k1 tbl] twice in next st—4 sts, sl same 4 sts back to LH needle, [k2tog] twice, lift 2nd st over first st on RH needle.

Row 1 (RS) K5, *yo, k1, [yo, ssk] twice, yo, k2, ssk, k5, k2tog, k2; rep from * to end.

Row 2 and all WS rows Purl.

Row 3 K5, *yo, k3, [yo, ssk] twice, yo, k2, ssk, k3, k2tog, k2; rep from * to end.

Row 5 K5, *yo, k2, MB, k2, [yo, ssk] twice, yo, k2, k2tog, k1, ssk, k2; rep from * to end.

Row 7 K5, *yo, k2, MB, k1, MB, k2, [yo, ssk] twice, yo, k2, sl 1-k2tog-psso, k2; rep from * to end.

Row 9. K2, *ssk, k5, k2tog, k2, [yo, k2tog] twice, yo, k1, yo, k2; rep from *, end k3.

Row 11 K2, *ssk, k3, k2tog, k2, [yo, ssk] twice, yo, k3, yo, k2; rep from *, end k3.

Row 13 K2, *ssk, k1, k2tog, k2, [yo, k2tog] twice, yo, k2, MB, k2, yo, k2; rep from *, end k3.

Row 15 K2, *sl 1-k2tog-psso, k2, [yo, k2tog] twice, yo, k2, MB, k1, MB, k2, yo, k2; rep from *, end k3.

Row 16 Purl.

Rep rows 1–16.

152 vines and eyelet rib

(multiple of 10 sts plus 5)

Row 1 (RS) K1, *ssk, yo, k5, k2tog, yo, k1; rep from *, end ssk, yo, k2.
Row 2 P1, *p2tog, yo, p2, yo, p1, p2tog, p3; rep from *, end p2tog, yo, p2.
Row 3 K1, *ssk, yo, k3, k2tog, k2, yo, k1; rep from *, end ssk, yo, k2.
Row 4 P1, *p2tog, yo, p2, yo, p3, p2tog, p1; rep from *, end p2tog, yo, p2.
Row 5 K1, *ssk, yo, k2, ssk, k3, yo, k1; rep from *, end ssk, yo, k2.
Row 6 P1, *p2tog, yo, p2, yo, p3, p2tog tbl, p1; rep from *, end p2tog, yo, p2.
Row 7 K1, *ssk, yo, k2, yo, ssk, k4; rep from *, end ssk, yo, k2.
Row 8 P1, *p2tog, yo, p4, p2tog tbl, p1, yo, p1; rep from *, end p2tog, yo, p2.
Row 9 K1, *ssk, [yo, k2] twice, ssk, k2; rep from *, end ssk, yo, k2.
Row 10 P1, *p2tog, yo, p2, p2tog tbl, p3, yo, p1; rep from *, end p2tog, yo, p2.
Row 11 K1, *ssk, yo, k2, yo, k3, k2tog, k1; rep from *, end ssk, yo, k2.
Row 12 P1, *p2tog, yo, p2, p2tog, p3, yo, p1; rep from *, end p2tog, yo, p2.
Rep rows 1–12.

152

153 ears of corn

(multiple of 19 sts plus 2)

Rows 1, 5, 9, 13 K1, *SKP, k2, yo, p1, yo, sl 1-k2tog-psso, yo, p3, yo, sl 1-k2tog-psso, yo, p1, yo, k2, k2tog; rep from *, end k1.
Rows 2, 4, 6, 8, 10, 12, 14 K1, * p4, k1, p3, k3, p3, k1, p4; rep from *, end k1.
Rows 3, 7, 11, 15 K1, * SKP, yo, k2, p1, yo, sl 1-k2tog-psso, yo, p3, yo, sl 1-k2tog-psso, yo, p1, k2, yo, k2tog; rep from *, end k1.
Rows 16, 18, 20, 22 K1, * p4, k2, p3, k1, p3, k2, p4; rep from *, end k1.
Rows 17, 21 K1, *SKP, k2, yo, p2, yo, sl 1-k2tog-psso, yo, p1, yo, sl 1-k2tog-psso, yo, p2, yo, k2, k2tog; rep from *, end k1.
Row 19 K1, *SKP, yo, k2, p2, sl 4 sts to cn and hold in *front*, yo, sl 1-k2tog-psso, yo, sl 1 st from LH side of cn to LH needle and p1, yo, sl 3 remaining sts from cn to LH needle, sl 1-k2tog-psso, yo, p2, k2, yo, k2tog; rep from *, end k1.
Row 23 Rep row 3.
Row 24 Rep row 2.
Rep rows 1–24.

153

(multiple of 34 sts plus 2)

Row 1 (RS) K1, *yo, ssk, k2, yo, ssk, p2, yo, k4, ssk, k6, k2tog, k4, yo, p2, k2, yo, ssk, k2; rep from *, end k1.

Row 2 K1, *yo, p2tog, p2, yo, p2tog, k2, p1, yo, p4, p2tog, p4, p2tog tbl, p4, yo, p1, k2, p2, yo, p2tog, p2; rep from *, end k1.

Row 3 K1, *yo, ssk, k2, yo, ssk, p2, k2, yo, k4, ssk, k2, k2tog, k4, yo, k2, p2, k2, yo, ssk, k2; rep from *, end k1.

Row 4 K1, *yo, p2tog, p2, yo, p2tog, k2, p3, yo, p4, p2tog, p2tog tbl, p4, yo, p3, k2, p2, yo, p2tog, p2; rep from *, end k1.

Rows 5-12 Rep row 1–4 twice more.

Row 13 K1, *k3, k2tog, k4, yo, p2, [k2, yo, ssk] 3 times, p2, yo, k4, ssk, k3; rep from *, end k1.

Row 14 K1, *p2, p2tog tbl, p4, yo, p1, k2, [p2, yo, p2tog] 3 times, k2, p1, yo, p4, p2tog, p2; rep from *, end k1.

Row 15 K1, *k1, k2tog, k4, yo, k2, p2, [k2, yo, ssk] 3 times, p2, k2, yo, k4, ssk, k1; rep from *, end k1.

Row 16 K1, *p2tog tbl, p4, yo, p3, k2, [p2, yo, p2tog] 3 times, k2, p3, yo, p4, p2tog; rep from *, end k1.

Rows 17-24 Rep rows 13-16 twice more.

Rep rows 1–24.

155 scalloped eyelet edging

(worked over 14sts)

Row 1 (WS) K2, yo, k2tog, k5, yo, k2tog, yo, k3.

Row 2 and all RS rows K1, yo, k2tog, k to end.

Row 3 K2, yo, k2tog, k4, [yo, k2tog] twice, yo, k3.

Row 5 K2, yo, k2tog, k3, [yo, k2tog] 3 times, yo, k3.

Row 7 K2, yo, k2tog, k2, [yo, k2tog] 4 times, yo, k3.

Row 9 K2, yo, k2tog, k1, [yo, k2tog] 5 times, yo, k3.

Row 11 K2, yo, k2tog, k1, k2tog, [yo, k2tog] 5 times, k2.

Row 13 K2, yo, k2tog, k2, k2tog, [yo, k2tog] 4 times, k2.

Row 15 K2, yo, k2tog, k3, k2tog, [yo, k2tog] 3 times, k2.

Row 17 K2, yo, k2tog, k4, k2tog, [yo, k2tog] twice, k2.

Row 19 K2, yo, k2tog, k5, k2tog, yo, k2tog, k2.

Row 20 Rep row 2.

Rep rows 1–20.

155

156 vines and bobbles

(cast on a multiple of 12 sts plus 1; multiple of 16 sts after Row 1)

MB (make bobble)

[K1, yo, k1, yo, k1] in next st (5 sts made), turn and k5, turn and p5, turn and k1, sl1-k2tog-psso, k1, turn and p3tog.

Row 1 (RS) *K5, yo, k1, yo, k3, k2tog; rep from * to end.

Rows 2, 4, 6 and 8 *P2tog, p10; rep from * to end.

Row 3 *K6, yo, k1, yo, k2, k2tog; rep from * to end.

Row 5 *K7, [yo, k1] twice, k2tog; rep from * to end.

Row 7 *K8, yo, k1, yo, k2tog; rep from * to end.

Row 9 *Ssk, k4, yo, k1, yo, k2, MB, k1; rep from * to end.

Row 10 Being sure to p into back of each bobble st, work as foll: *p10, p2tog tbl; rep from * to end.

Row 11 *Ssk, k3, yo, k1, yo, k5; rep from * to end.

Rows 12, 14, 16 and 18 *P10, p2tog tbl; rep from * to end.

Row 13 *Ssk, k2, yo, k1, yo, k6; rep from * to end.

Row 15 *Ssk, [k1, yo] twice, k7; rep from * to end.

Row 17 *Ssk, yo, k1, yo, k8; rep from * to end.

Row 19 *K1, MB, k2, yo, k1, yo, k4, k2tog; rep from * to end.

Row 20 *P2tog, p10; rep from * to end.

Rep rows 1–20.

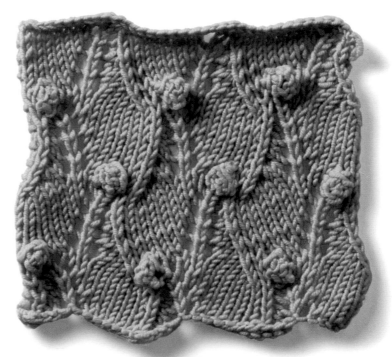

157 georgia lace

(multiple of 14 sts plus 1)

Row 1 K4, *yo, k7; rep from *, end yo, k4.

Row 2 and all WS rows Purl

Row 3 K2, *k2tog, yo, k2tog, k5, SKP, yo, SKP, k3; rep from *, end last rep k2.

Row 5 *K1, k2tog, yo, k2tog, k5, SKP, yo, SKP, rep from *, end k1.

Row 7 K2tog, *yo, k2tog, k2, yo, k1, yo, k2, SKP, yo, k3tog; rep from *, end last rep k2tog.

Row 9 *K1, yo, k2tog, k2, yo, k3, yo, k2, SKP, yo; rep from *, end k1.

Row 11 *K1, k2tog, k2, yo, k5, yo, k2, SKP; rep from *, end k1.

Row 13 Rep row 1.

Row 15 *K1, yo, k2, SKP, yo, k7, yo, k2tog, k2, yo; rep from *, end k1.

Row 17 k2, *yo, k2, SKP, yo, SKP, k3, k2tog, yo, k2tog, k2, yo, k3; rep from *, end last rep k2.

Row 19 K3, *yo, k2, SKP, yo, SKP, k1, k2tog, yo, k2tog, k2, yo, k5; rep from *, end last rep k3.

Row 21 K4, *yo, k2, SKP, yo, k3tog, yo, k2tog, k2, yo, k7; rep from *, end last rep k4.

Row 23 K4, *yo, k2tog, k1, SKP, yo, k1, yo, k2tog, k1, SKP, yo, k7; rep from *, end last rep k4.

Row 25 K2, *k2tog, yo, k2tog, k1, SKP, k1, k2tog, k1, SKP, yo, SKP, k3; rep from *, end last rep k2.

Row 26 Purl.

Rep rows 5–2.

traveling

158 open chevron

(multiple of 12 sts)

RT (right twist) Sl next st to cn and hold to back, k1, k1 from cn.

LT (left twist) Sl next st to cn and hold to front, k1, k1 from cn.

RPT (right purl twist) Sl next st to cn and hold to back, k1, p1 from cn.

LPT (left purl twist) Sl next st to cn and hold to front, p1, k1 from cn.

Rows 1, 3 and 5 (RS) Knit.

Rows 2, 4 and 6 Purl.

Row 7 *LPT, k8, RPT; rep from * to end.

Row 8 *K1, p10, k1; rep from * to end.

Row 9 *P1, LPT, k6, RPT, p1; rep from * to end.

Row 10 *K2, p8, k2; rep from * to end.

Row 11 *P2, LPT, k4, RPT, p2; rep from * to end.

Row 12 *K3, p6, k3; rep from * to end.

Row 13 *P3, LPT, k2, RPT, p3; rep from * to end.

Row 14 *K4, p4, k4; rep from * to end.

Row 15 *P4, LPT, RPT, p4; rep from * to end.

Row 16 *K5, p2, k5; rep from * to end.

Row 17 *P5, RPT, p5; rep from * to end.

Rows 18, 20, 22 and 24 Knit.

Rows 19, 21 and 23 Purl.

Row 25 *P5, RT, p5; rep from * to end.

Row 26 *K5, p2, k5; rep from * to end.

Row 27 *P4, RT, LT, p4; rep from * to end.

Row 28 *K4, p4, k4; rep from * to end.

Row 29 *P3, RT, k2, LT, p3; rep from * to end.

Row 30 *K3, p6, k3; rep from * to end.

Row 31 *P2, RT, k4, LT, p2; rep from * to end.

Row 32 *K2, p8, k2; rep from * to end.

Row 33 *P1, RT, k6, LT, p1; rep from * to end.

Row 34 *K1, p10, k1; rep from * to end.

Row 35 *RT, k8, LT; rep from * to end.

Row 36 Purl.

Rep rows 1–36.

158

159 stockinette chevron

(multiple of 6 sts)

Rows 1 and 3 (RS) Knit.

Row 2 (WS) Purl.

Row 4 *P5, k1; rep from * to end.

Row 5 *K1, p1, k3, p1; rep from * to end.

Row 6 *[P1, k1] twice, p2; rep from * to end.

Row 7 K3, *p1, k5; rep from *, end k2.

Rows 8 and 10 Purl.

Row 9 Knit.

Row 11 *P1, k5; rep from * to end.

Row 12 *K1, p3, k1, p1; rep from * to end.

Row 13 *K2, [p1, k1] twice; rep from * to end.

Row 14 P2, *k1, p5; rep from *, end p3.

Row 15 Knit.

Row 16 Purl .

Row 17 Knit.

160 stockinette window pane

(multiple of 12 sts plus 1)

Row 1 (RS) *K6, p1, k5; rep from *, end k1.

Row 2 P1, *p4, k1, p1, k1, p5; rep from * to end.

Row 3 *K4, p1, k3, p1, k3; rep from *, end k1.

Row 4 P1, *p2, k1, p5, k1, p3; rep from * to end.

Row 5 *K2, p1, k7, p1, k1; rep from *, end k1.

Row 6 P1, *k1, p9, k1, p1; rep from * to end.

Row 7 *P1, k11; rep from *, end p1.

Row 8 Rep row 6.

Row 9 Rep row 5.

Row 10 Rep row 4.

Row 11 Rep row 3.

Row 12 Rep row 2.

Rep rows 1–12.

159

160

161 chevron stripes

(multiple of 18 sts)

Row 1 *K6, p3, k7, p1, k1; rep from * to end.

Row 2 *K3, p7, k1, p7; rep from * to end.

Row 3 *P1, k13, p4; rep from * to end.

Row 4 *K5, p11, k2; rep from * to end.

Row 5 *P3, k9, p6; rep from * to end.

Row 6 *K7, p7, k4; rep from * to end.

Row 7 *P5, k5, p8; rep from * to end.

Row 8 *K9, p3, k6; rep from * to end.

Row 9 *P7, k1, p8, k1, p1; rep from * to end.

Row 10 *P3, k15; rep from * to end.

Row 11 *K1, p13, k4; rep from * to end.

Row 12 *P5, k11, p2; rep from * to end.

Row 13 *K3, p9, k6; rep from * to end.

Row 14 *P7, k7, p4; rep from * to end.

Row 15 *K5, p5, k8; rep from * to end.

Row 16 *P1, k1, p7, k3, p6; rep from * to end.

Row 17 *K7, p1, k7, p3; rep from * to end.

Row 18 *K4, p13, k1; rep from * to end.

Row 19 *P2, k11, p5; rep from * to end.

Row 20 *K6, p9, k3; rep from * to end.

Row 21 *P4, k7, p7; rep from * to end.

Row 22 *K8, p5, k5; rep from * to end.

Row 23 *P6, k3, p9; rep from * to end.

Row 24 *K1, p1, k8, p1, k7; rep from * to end.

Row 25 *P15, k3; rep from * to end.

Row 26 *P4, k13, p1; rep from * to end.

Row 27 *K2, p11, k5; rep from * to end.

Row 28 *P6, k9, p3; rep from * to end.

Row 29 *K4, p7, k7; rep from * to end.

Row 30 *P8, k5, p5; rep from * to end.

Rep rows 1–30.

161

162 diagonal basketweave

(multiple of 18 sts)

Row 1 (RS) *K2, p7, k1, p7, k1; rep from * to end.

Row 2 *K7, p3, k7, p1; rep from * to end.

Row 3 *P7, k5, p5, k1; rep from * to end.

Row 4 *K1, p1, k3, p7, k6; rep from * to end.

Row 5 *P5, k9, p1, k1, p2; rep from * to end.

Row 6 *K3, p11, k4; rep from * to end.

Row 7 *P3, k1, p1, k9, p4; rep from * to end.

Row 8 *K5, p7, k3, p1, k2; rep from * to end.

Row 9 *P1, k1, p5, k5, p6; rep from * to end.

Row 10 *K7, p3, k7, p1; rep from * to end.

Row 11 *K2, p7, k1, p7, k1; rep from * to end.

Row 12 *P2, k5, p1, k7, p3; rep from * to end.

Row 13 *K4, p7, k1, p3, k3; rep from * to end.

Row 14 *P4, k1, p1, k7, p5; rep from * to end.

Row 15 *K6, p7, k5; rep from * to end.

Row 16 *P4, k7, p1, k1, p5; rep from * to end.

Row 17 *K4, p3, k1, p7, k3; rep from * to end.

Row 18 *P2, k7, p1, k5, p3; rep from * to end.

Rep rows 1–18.

162

163 moss stitch diamonds

(multiple of 16 sts)

Row 1 (RS) K2, *p2, k1, p2, k2, p2, k1, p2, k4; rep from *, end k2.
Row 2 P2, *k2, p1, k2, p2, k2, p1, k2, p4; rep from *, end p2.
Row 3 K3, *p2, k2, p2, k2, p2, k6; rep from *, end k3.
Row 4 P4, *k2, p1, k2, p1, k2, p8; rep from *, end p4.
Row 5 K5, *p2, k2, p2, k10; rep from *, end k5.
Row 6 P6, *k4, p12; rep from *, end p6.
Row 7 K7, *p2, k14; rep from *, end k7.
Row 8 K1, *p14, k2; rep from *, end k1.
Row 9 P2, *k12, p4; rep from *, end p2.
Row 10 P1, *k2, p10, k2, p2; rep from *, end p1.
Row 11 P1, *k1, p2, k8, p2, k1, p2; rep from *, end p1.
Row 12 K1, *p2, k2, p6, k2, p2, k2; rep from *, end k1.
Row 13 K1, *p2, k1, p2, k4, p2, k1, p2, k2; rep from *, end k1.
Row 14 P1, *k2, p1, k2, p4, k2, p1, k2, p2; rep from *, end p1.
Row 15 P1, *k2, p2, k6, p2, k2, p2; rep from *, end p1.
Row 16 K1, *p1, k2, p8, k2, p1, k2; rep from *, end k1.
Row 17 K1, *p2, k10, p2, k2; rep from *, end k1.
Row 18 K2, *p12, k4; rep from *, end k2.
Row 19 P1, *k14, p2; rep from *, end p1.
Row 20 P7, *k2, p14; rep from *, end p7.
Row 21 K6, *p4, k12; rep from *, end k6.
Row 22 P5, *k2, p2, k2, p10; rep from *, end p5.
Row 23 K4, *p2, k1, p2, k1, p2, k8; rep from *, end k4.
Row 24 P3, *k2, p2, k2, p2, k2, p6; rep from *, end p3.
Rep rows 1–24.

163

164 parquet pattern

(multiple of 18 sts)

Row 1 (RS) *K3, p2, k3, p3, k4, p2, k1; rep from * to end.

Row 2 *K2, p4, [k2, p1] twice, k2, p4; rep from * to end.

Row 3 *P1, k4, p3, k3, p2, k4, p1; rep from * to end.

Row 4 *P4, k3, p4, k2, p3, k2; rep from * to end.

Row 5 *[K1, p2] twice, k4, p2, k1, p2, k3; rep from * to end.

Row 6 *P2, k2, p3, k2, p4, k3, p2; rep from * to end.

Row 7 *K2, p2, k4, p2, k4, p3, k1; rep from * to end.

Row 8 *K2, p1, [k2, p4] twice, k2, p1; rep from * to end.

Row 9 *[P2, k4] twice, p2, k3, p1; rep from * to end.

Row 10 *K1, [p4, k2] twice, p3, k2; rep from * to end.

Row 11 *[K1, p2] twice, [k4, p2] twice; rep from * to end.

Row 12 *P1, [k2, p4] twice, k3, p2; rep from * to end.

Row 13 *[K3, p2] twice, k4, p3, k1; rep from * to end.

Row 14 *K2, p1, k2, p4, k2, p1, k2, p4; rep from * to end.

Row 15 *P1, k4, p3, k4, p2, k3, p1; rep from * to end.

Row 16 *P4, k3, p3, k2, p4, k2; rep from * to end.

Row 17 *K1, p2, k4, [p2, k1] twice, p2, k3; rep from * to end.

Row 18 *P2, k2, p3, k3, p4, k2, p2; rep from * to end.

Rep rows 1–18.

165 little chevrons

(multiple of 6 sts)

Rows 1 and 3 (RS) Purl.

Row 2 Knit.

Row 4 *K5, p1; rep from * to end.

Row 5 *K1, p5; rep from * to end.

Row 6 P1, *k3, p3; rep from *, end p2.

Row 7 K2, *p3, k3; rep from *, end k1.

Row 8 *P2, k1; rep from * to end.

Row 9 *P1, k2; rep from * to end.

Row 10 K1, *p3, k3; rep from *, end k2.

Row 11 P2, *k3, p3; rep from *, end p1.

Row 12 K2, *p1, k5; rep from *, end k3.

Row 13 P3, *k1, p5; rep from *, end p2.

Row 14 Knit.

Row 15 Purl.

Row 16 Knit.

Rep rows 1–16.

166 arrow stripe

(multiple of 8 sts)

Rows 1–6 Knit.

Row 7 (RS) *K4, p4; rep from * to end.

Row 8 P1, *k4, p4; rep from *, end p3.

Row 9 K2, *p4, k4; rep from *, end k2.

Row 10 P3, *k4, p4; rep from *, end p1.

Row 11 *P4, k4; rep from * to end.

Row 12 K1, *p4, k4; rep from *, end k3.

Rows 13 and 15 K3, *p4, k4; rep from *, end k1.

Rows 14 and 16 P1, *k4, p4; rep from *, end p3.

Row 17 P3, *k4, p4; rep from *, end p1.

Row 18 *P4, k4; rep from * to end.

Row 19 K1, *p4, k4; rep from *, end k3.

Row 20 P2, *k4, p4; rep from *, end p2.

Row 21 K3, *p4, k4; rep from *, end k1.

Row 22 *K4, p4; rep from * to end.

Rows 23–28 Knit.

Rep rows 1–28.

167 diagonal stripes

(multiple of 27 sts)

Row 1 (RS) *K2, p3, k3, p3, k6, p3, k3, p3, k1; rep from * to end.

Row 2 *P2, k3, p3, k3, p3, k1, p2, k3, p3, k3, p1; rep from * to end.

Row 3 *P3, k3, p3, k3, p2, k3, p1, k3, p3, k3; rep from * to end.

Row 4 *K1, p3, k3, p5, k3, p4, k3, p3, k2; rep from * to end.

Row 5 *P1, k3, p3, k2, p1, k3, p3, k3, p3, k3, p2; rep from * to end.

Row 6 *K3, p3, k1, p3, k3, p3, k2, p3, k3, p3; rep from * to end.

Row 7 *K2, p3, k4, p3, k3, p3, k5, p3, k1; rep from * to end.

Row 8 *P2, k3, p3, k3, p3, k3, p3, k1, p2, k3, p1; rep from * to end.

Row 9 *P3, k3, p2, k3, p3, k3, p3, k3, p1, k3; rep from * to end.

Row 10 *K1, p5, k3, p3, k3, p3, k3, p4, k2; rep from * to end.

Row 11 *P1, k6, p3, k3, p3, k3, p3, k3, p2; rep from * to end.

Row 12 *K1, p3, k3, p3, k3, p3, k3, p8; rep from * to end.

Row 13 *K5, p1, k3, p3, k3, p3, k3, p3, k3; rep from * to end.

Row 14 *P2, k3, p3, k3, p3, k3, p3, k3, p4; rep from * to end.

Row 15 *K3, p3, k5, p3, k3, p3, k3, p3, k1; rep from * to end.

Row 16 *K3, p3, k3, p3, k3, p3, k1, p3, k3, p2; rep from * to end.

Row 17 *K1, p3, k3, p3, k3, p3, k3, p3, k3, p1, k1; rep from * to end.

Row 18 *P4, k3, p3, k3, p5, k3, p3, k3; rep from * to end.

Row 19 *P2, k3, p3, k3, p1, k3, p3, k3, p1, k4, p1; rep from * to end.

Row 20 *K2, p6, k3, p3, k3, p3, k3, p3, k1; rep from * to end.

Row 21 *K3, p3, k3, p3, k5, p3, k4, p3; rep from * to end.

Row 22 *P1, k3, p4, k1, p3, k1, p3, k3, p3, k3, p2; rep from * to end.

Row 23 *K1, p3, k3, p3, k3, p3, k6, p3, k2; rep from * to end.

Row 24 *P3, k3, p6, k3, p3, k3, p3, k3; rep from * to end.

Row 25 *P2, k3, p3, k3, p3, k6, p3, k3, p1; rep from * to end.

Row 26 *K2, p3, k3, p6, k3, p3, k3, p3, k1; rep from * to end.

Row 27 *K3, p3, k3, p3, k6, p3, k3, p3; rep from * to end.

167

168 infinite chevron

(multiple of 16 sts plus 1)

Note Place markers on either side of center st. Directions for RS rows are divided in half—before markers (*) and after markers (+)

Row 1 (RS) *P5, k3; rep from * to first marker, sm, p1, sm, +k3, p5; rep from + to end.

Row 2 and all WS rows K the knit sts and p the purl sts.

Row 3 P4, *k3, p5; rep from * to first marker, end p1, sm, p1, sm, p1, k3, +p5, k3; rep from +, end p4.

Row 5 P3, *k3, p5; rep from * to first marker, end p2, sm, p1, sm, p2, k3, +p5, k3; rep from +, end p3.

Row 7 P2, *k3, p5; rep from * to first marker, end p3, sm, p1, sm, p3, k3, +p5, k3; rep from +, end p2.

Row 9 P1, *k3, p5; rep from * to first marker, end p4, sm, p1, sm, p4, k3, +p5, k3; rep from +, end p1.

Row 11 *K3, p5; rep from * to first marker, sm, k1, sm, +p5, k3; rep from + to end.

Row 13 K2, p5, *k3, p5; rep from * to first marker, end k1, sm, k1, sm, k1, p5, +k3, p5; rep from +, end k2.

Row 15 K1, p5, *k3, p5, rep from * to first marker, end k2, sm, k1, sm, k2, +p5, k3; rep from +, end k1.

Row 16 K the knits sts and p the purl sts.

Rep rows 1–16.

169 twisted stitch triangles

(multiple of 18 sts)

Rows 1 and 3 (RS) *K1, p2, [k1 tbl, p1] 3 times, p2, [k1 tbl, p1] 3 times, p1; rep from * to end.

Rows 2 and 4 *K2, [p1 tbl, k1] 3 times, k2, [p1 tbl, k1] 3 times, k1, p1; rep from * to end.

Rows 5 and 7 *K2, p2, [k1 tbl, p1] 6 times, p1, k1; rep from * to end.

Rows 6 and 8 *P1, k2, [p1 tbl, k1] 6 times, k1, p2; rep from * to end.

Rows 9 and 11 *K3, p2, [k1 tbl, p1] 5 times, p1, k2; rep from * to end.

Rows 10 and 12 *P2, k2, [p1tbl, k1] 5 times, k1, p3; rep from * to end.

Rows 13 and 15 *P1, k3, p2, [k1 tbl, p1] 4 times, p1, k3; rep from * to end.

Rows 14 and 16 *P3, k2, [p1 tbl, k1] 4 times, k1, p3, k1; rep from * to end.

Rows 17 and 19 *P2, k3, p2, [k1 tbl, p1] 3 times, p1, k3, p1; rep from * to end.

Rows 18 and 20 *K1, p3, k2, [p1 tbl, k1] 3 times, k1, p3, k2; rep from * to end.

Rows 21 and 23 *K1 tbl, p2, k3, p2, k1 tbl, p1, k1 tbl, p2, k3, p2; rep from * to end.

Rows 22 and 24 *K2, p3, k2, p1 tbl, k1, p1 tbl, k2, p3, k2, p1 tbl; rep from * to end.

Rows 25 and 27 *P1, k1 tbl, p2, k3, p2, k1 tbl, p2, k3, p2, k1 tbl; rep from * to end.

Rows 26 and 28 *P1 tbl, k2, p3, k2, p1 tbl, k2, p3, k2, p1 tbl, k1; rep from * to end.

Rows 29 and 31 *K1 tbl, p1, k1 tbl, p2, k3, p3, k3, p2, k1 tbl, p1; rep from * to end.

Rows 30 and 32 *K1, p1 tbl, k2, p3, k3, p3, k2, p1 tbl, k1, p1 tbl; rep from * to end.

Rows 33 and 35 *[P1, k1 tbl] twice, p2, k3, p1, k3, p2, k1 tbl, p1, k1 tbl; rep from * to end.

Rows 34 and 36 *[P1 tbl, k1] twice, k1, p3, k1, p3, k2, [p1 tbl, k1] twice; rep from * to end.

Rows 37 and 39 *[K1 tbl, p1] 3 times, p1, k5, p2, [k1 tbl, p1] twice; rep from * to end.

Rows 38 and 40 *[K1, p1 tbl] twice, k2, p5, k1, [k1, p1 tbl] 3 times; rep from * to end.

Rows 41 and 43 *[P1, k1 tbl] 3 times, p2, k3, p1, [p1, k1 tbl] 3 times; rep from * to end.

Rows 42 and 44 *[P1 tbl, k1] 3 times, k1, p3, k2, [p1 tbl, k1] 3 times; rep from * to end.

Rows 45 and 47 *P2, [k1 tbl, p1] 3 times, p1, k1, p2, [k1 tbl, p1] 3 times; rep from * to end.

Rows 46 and 48 *[K1, p1 tbl] 3 times, k2, p1, k2, [p1 tbl, k1] 3 times, k1; rep from * to end.

Rep rows 1–48.

169

170 diagonal moss stripe

(multiple of 12 sts)
Row 1 (RS) *P1, k5, p1, k2, p1, k1, p1; rep from * to end.
Row 2 *P1, k1, p3, k2, p4, k1; rep from * to end.
Row 3 *P1, k3, p1, k1, p1, k4, p1; rep from * to end.
Row 4 *P5, k2, p1, k1, p2, k1; rep from * to end.
Row 5 *K2, [p1, k1] twice, p1, k5; rep from * to end.
Row 6 *P6, [k1, p1] 3 times; rep from * to end.
Row 7 *[P1, k1] twice, p1, k7; rep from * to end.
Row 8 *P5, k1, p2, k1, p1, k2; rep from * to end.
Row 9 *P1, k1, p1, k3, p2, k4; rep from * to end.
Row 10 *P3, k1, p1, k1, p4, k2; rep from * to end.
Row 11 *P1, k5, p2, k1, p1, k2; rep from * to end.
Row 12 *[P1, k1] 3 times, p6; rep from * to end.
Row 13 *K7, [p1, k1] twice, p1; rep from * to end.
Row 14 *[P1, k1] twice, p7, k1; rep from * to end.
Rep rows 1–14.

171 chevron rib

(multiple of 18 sts plus 1)
Rows 1 and 3 (RS) P1, *[k2, p2] twice, k1, [p2, k2] twice, p1; rep from * to end.
Rows 2 and 4 *K1, [p2, k2] twice, p1, [k2, p2] twice; rep from *, end k1.
Rows 5 and 7 P1, *p1, [k2, p2] twice, k1, [k2, p2] twice; rep from * to end.
Rows 6 and 8 *[K2, p2] twice, k3, p2, k2, p2, k1; rep from *, end k1.
Rows 9 and 11 K1, *[p2, k2] twice, p1, [k2, p2] twice, k1; rep from * to end.
Rows 10 and 12 *P1, [k2, p2] twice, k1, [p2, k2] twice; rep from *, end p1.
Rows 13 and 15 K1, *k1, [p2, k2] twice, k1, [p2, k2] twice; rep from * to end.
Rows 14 and 16 *[P2, k2] twice, p3, k2, p2, k2, p1; rep from *, end p1.
Rep rows 1–16.

170

171

172 alternating diagonals

(multiple of 10 sts)

Rows 1 and 3 (RS) *K5, p5; rep from * to end.

Row 2 and all WS rows K the knit sts and p the purl sts.

Row 5 *K4, p1, k1, p4; rep from * to end.

Row 7 *K3, p2, k2, p3; rep from * to end.

Row 9 *K2, p3, k3, p2; rep from * to end.

Row 11 *K1, p4, k4, p1; rep from * to end.

Rows 13 and 15 *P5, k5; rep from * to end.

Row 17 *P4, k1, p1, k4; rep from * to end.

Row 19 *P3, k2, p2, k3; rep from * to end.

Row 21 *P2, k3, p3, k2; rep from * to end.

Row 23 *P1, k4, p4, k1; rep from * to end.

Row 24 Rep row 2.

Rep rows 1–24.

173 diagonal shadow stripes

(multiple of 4 sts plus 2)

p1-b (p 1 in row below)

Row 1 and all WS rows Knit.

Row 2 (RS) P1, p1-b, p3; rep from *, end p1.

Row 4 P2, p1-b, p3; rep from * to end.

Row 6 P3, p1-b, p3; rep from *, end last rep p2.

Row 8 P4, p1-b, p3; rep from *, end last rep p1.

Rep rows 1–8.

172

173

174 woven tile

(multiple of 6 sts plus 2)

Rows 1 and 3 (WS) Wrapping yarn twice around needle for each st, purl across.

Row 2 Letting extra wrap drop for each st, work across as foll: K1, *sl next 3 sts to cn and hold to *back*, k3, k3 from cn; rep from *, end k1.

Row 4 Letting extra wrap drop for each st, work across as foll: k4, *sl next 3 sts to cn and hold to *front*, k3, k3 from cn: rep from *, end k4.

Rep rows 1–4.

175 herringbone linen

(multiple of 4 sts plus 2)

Rows 1, 5, 9, 15, 19, 23 (RS) K1, *wyif sl 2, k2; rep from *, end k1.

Rows 2, 6, 10, 14, 18, 22 K1, *p1, wyib sl 2, p1; rep from *, end k1.

Rows 3, 7, 11, 13, 17, 21 K1, *k2,wyif sl 2; rep from *, end k1.

Rows 4, 8, 12, 16, 20 K1, *wyib sl 1, p2, wyib sl 1; rep from *, end k1.

Row 24 K1, *wyib sl 1, p2, wyib sl 1; rep from *, end k1.

Rep rows 1–24.

174

175

176 right slant rib

(multiple of 6 sts plus 4)

4-st RP (4-st right purl twist) Sl 3 sts to cn and hold to *back*, k1, wyif sl the 2 purl sts from cn back to LH needle and p these 2 sts, then k the rem st from cn.

Rows 1, 3, 5 and 7 (WS) P1, *k2, p1; rep from * to end.

Rows 2 and 6 K1, *p2, k1; rep from * to end.

Row 4 *4-st RPT, p2; rep from *, end 4-st RPT.

Row 8 K1, p2, *4st RPT, p2; rep from *, end k1.

Rep rows 1–8.

177 diagonal stripe rib

(multiple of 7 sts plus 1)

RT (right twist) Sl next st to cn and hold to *back*, k1, k1 from cn.

Rows 1 and 3 (WS) *K1, p6; rep from *, end k1.

Row 2 P1, *RT 3 times, p1; rep from * to end.

Row 4 P1, *k1, RT twice, k1, p1; rep from * to end.

Rep rows 1–4.

traveling

176

177

178 gulls and garter

(multiple of 8 sts plus 1)
Rows 1 and 3 (WS) K2, *p5, k3; rep from *, end last rep k2.
Row 2 K2, *wyif sl 5 sts purlwise, k3; rep from *, end last rep k2.
Row 4 K4, *insert RH needle under strand 2 rows below, k next st
on LH needle, drawing loop through st on needle and under
strand in one motion, k7; rep from *, end last rep k4.
Rep rows 1–4.

179 palm leaves

(multiple of 7 sts plus 1)
Inc 1 (increase one) With RH needle behind LH needle,
insert tip of RH needle from top down into loop of purled
st of row below, k this st, then k st on LH needle.
Rows 1 and 3 (WS) Purl.
Row 2 *K2tog, k2, inc 1, k2; rep from *, end k1.
Row 4 K1, *k2, inc 1, k2, k2tog; rep from * to end.
Rep rows 1–4.

178

179

180 split palm leaves

(multiple of 11 sts plus 2)
Row 1 (RS) K1, *k2tog, k3, M1, k1, M1, k3, ssk; rep from *, end k1.
Row 2 Purl.
Rep rows 1 and 2.

181 laddered columns

(multiple of 11 sts plus 3)
dvd (double vertical decrease) Sl next 2 sts to RH needle as if to k2tog, k next st, pass 2 slipped sts over k1.
Foundation row Purl.
Row 1 (RS) K1, k2tog, k4, yo twice, k4, *dvd, k4, yo twice, k4; rep from * to last 3 sts, k2tog, k1.
Row 2 P6, [p1, k1] in yos of previous row, *p9, [p1, k1] in yos of previous row; rep from * to last 6 sts, p6.
Rep rows 1 and 2.

180

181

182 ribbed leaves

(multiple of 22 sts)

R2dec (right double increase)
Sl p st to RH needle, sl k st to cn and hold to front of work, sl next p st to RH needle, sl k st from cn back to LH needle, sl 2 p sts back to LH needle, p2tog, k2tog.

L2dec (left double increase)
Wyib, sl k st to RH needle knitwise, sl p st to cn and hold to back of work, sl next k st to RH needle knitwise, sl p from cn back to LH needle. Leaving 2 k sts on RH needle, ssk, p next 2 sts on LH needle tog.

Rows 1, 3, 5 and 7 (RS) *K1, p1, yo twice, [k1, p1] twice, k1, R2dec, [p1, k1] 5 times, p1; rep from * to end.

Row 2 and all WS rows work in k1, p1 rib, working double yo as 2 sts.

Rows 9, 11, 13 and 15 *[K1, p1] 6 times, L2dec, [k1, p1] twice, k1, yo twice, p1; rep from * to end.

Row 16 Rep row 2.

Rep rows 1–16.

183 diagonal eyelet inserts

(multiple of 14 sts)

RT (right twist) K2tog and leave on LH needle, k first st again and sl both sts off needle.

Row 1 (RS) K7, *k2tog, yo, RT, k10; rep from *, end k3.

Row 2 and all WS rows Purl.

Row 3 K6, *k2tog, yo, RT, k10; rep from *, end k4.

Row 5 K5, *k2tog, yo, RT, k10; rep from *, end k5.

Row 7 K4, *k2tog, yo, RT, k10; rep from *, end k6.

Row 9 K3, *k2tog, yo, RT, k10; rep from *, end k7.

Rows 11 and 13 Knit.

Rows 12 and 14 Purl.

Rep rows 1–14.

182

193

(worked over 44 sts)

Row 1 (RS) M1, [k2, p2] twice, k1, SKP, p1, [k2, p2] 4 times, k2, p1, k2tog, k1, [p2, k2] twice, M1.

Row 2 and all WS rows Purl.

Row 3 K1, M1, [k2, p2] twice, k1, SKP, [k2, p2] 4 times, k2, k2tog, k1, [p2, k2] twice, M1, k1.

Row 5 K2, M1 p-st, [k2, p2]twice, k1, SKP, k1, [p2, k2] 3 times, p2, k1, k2tog, k1, [p2, k2] twice, M1 p-st, k2.

Row 7 K2, p1, M1 p-st, [k2, p2] twice, k1, SKP, [p2, k2] 3 times, p2, k2tog, k1, [p2, k2] twice, M1 p-st, p1, k2.

Row 9 K2, p2, M1, [k2, p2] twice, k1, SKP, p1, [k2, p2] twice, k2, p1, k2tog, k1, [p2, k2] twice, M1, p2, k2.

Row 11 K2, p2, k1, M1, [k2, p2] twice, k1, SKP, [k2, p2] twice, k2, k2tog, k1, [p2, k2] twice, M1, k1, p2, k2.

Row 13 K2, p2, k2, M1 p-st, [k2, p2] twice, k1, SKP, k1, p2, k2, p2, k1, k2tog, k1, [p2, k2] twice, M1 p-st, k2, p2, k2.

Row 15 K2, p2, k2, p1, M1 p-st, [k2, p2] twice, k1, SKP, p2, k2, p2, k2tog, k1, [p2, k2] twice, M1 p-st, p1, k2, p2, k2.

Row 16 Purl.

Rep rows 1–16.

185 vertical zig zag

(multiple of 10 sts plus 2)

RI (raised inc) With RH needle behind LH needle, insert tip of RH needle from top down into lp of p st below, k this st leaving lp on needle, then knit next st on LH needle.

Row 1 K1, *RI, k2, ssk, k5; rep from *, end k1.

Row 2 and all WS rows K1, p to last st, k1.

Row 3 K1, *k1, RI, k2, ssk, k4; rep from *, end k1.

Row 5 K1, *k2, RI, k2, ssk, k3; rep from *, end k1.

Row 7 K1, *k3, RI, k2, ssk, k2; rep from *, end k1.

Row 9 K1, *k4, RI, k2, ssk, k1; rep from *, end k1.

Row 11 K1, *k5, RI, k2, ssk; rep from *, end k1.

Row 13 K1, *k5, k2tog, k2, RI; rep from *, end k1.

Row 15 K1, *k4, k2tog, k2, RI, k1; rep from *, end k1.

Row 17 K1, *k3, k2tog, k2, RI, k2; rep from *, end k1.

Row 19 K1, *k2, k2tog, k2, RI, k3; rep from *, end k1.

Row 21 K1, *k1, k2tog, k2, RI, k4; rep from *, end k1.

Row 23 K1, *k2tog, k2, RI, k5; rep from *, end k1.

Row 24 K1, p to last st, k1.

Rep rows 1–24.

185

186 eyelet leaves

(worked over 37 sts)

P2tog tbl (purl 2 tog through back loop) Slip next 2 sts knitwise one at a time to RH needle, slip them to LH needle, insert RH needle from left to right into back loops of the sts on LH needle and purl, then tog.

Row 1 (RS) Yo, k10, ssk, k9, k2tog, k9, yo, k5.

Row 2 P6, yo, p9, p2tog, p7, p2tog tbl, p10, yo, p1.

Row 3 K2, yo, k10, ssk, k5, k2tog, k9, yo, k7.

Row 4 P8, yo, p9, p2tog tbl, p3, p2tog tbl, p10, yo, p3.

Row 5 K4, yo, k10, ssk, k1, k2tog, k9, yo, k9.

Row 6 Yo, p9, p2tog, p9, p2tog tbl, p10, yo, p5.

Row 7 K6, yo, k10, ssk, k7, k2tog, k9, yo, k1.

Row 8 P2, yo, p9, p2tog, p5, p2tog tbl, p10, yo, p7.

Row 9 K8, yo, k10, ssk, k3, k2tog, k9, yo, k3.

Row 10 P4, yo, p9, p2tog, p1, p2tog tbl, p10, yo, p9.

Rep rows 1–10.

186

187 fan panels

(work over 34 sts)

Row 1 (RS) K2, M1, ssk, k4, k2tog, k3, M1, [k2, p1] twice, k2, M1, k3, ssk, k4, k2tog, M1, k2.

Row 2 and all WS rows Purl.

Row 3 K2, M1, k1, ssk, k2, k2tog, k4, M1, [k2, p1] twice, k2, M1, k4, ssk, k2, k2tog, k1, M1, k2.

Row 5 K2, M1, k2, ssk, k2tog, k5, M1, [k2, p1] twice, k2, M1, k5, ssk, k2tog, k2, M1, k2.

Row 7 K2, M1, k3, ssk, k4, k2tog, M1, [k2, p1] twice, k2, M1, ssk, k4, k2tog, k3, M1, k2.

Row 9 K2, M1, k4, ssk, k2, k2tog, k1, M1, [k2, p1] twice, k2, M1, k1, ssk, k2, k2tog, k4, M1, k2.

Row 11 K2, M1, k5, ssk, k2tog, k2, M1, [k2, p1] twice, k2, M1, k2, ssk, k2tog, k5, M1, k2.

Row 12 Purl.

Rep rows 1–12.

188 chevron panels

(multiple of 16 sts plus 3)

Row 1 (RS) *P3, M1, k3, p2, p3tog, p2, k3, M1; rep from *, end p3.

Row 2 K3, *p4, k5, p4, k3; rep from * to end.

Row 3 *P3, M1, k4, p1, p3tog, p1, k4, M1; rep from *, end p3.

Row 4 K3, *[p5, k3] twice; rep from * to end.

Row 5 *P3, M1, k5, p3tog, k5, M1; rep from *, end p3.

Row 6 K3, *p6, k1, p6, k3; rep from * to end.

Rep rows 1–6.

189 mock cable swirl

(multiple of 16 sts plus 2)

Row 1 (RS) P2, *yo, k3, ssk, k9, p2; rep from * to end.

Row 2 K2, *p8, p2tog tbl, p3, yo, p1, k2; rep from * to end.

Row 3 P2, *k2, yo, k3, ssk, k7, p2; rep from * to end.

Row 4 K2, *p6, p2tog tbl, p3, yo, p3, k2; rep from * to end.

Row 5 P2, *k4, yo, k3, ssk, k5, p2; rep from * to end.

Row 6 K2, *p4, p2tog tbl, p3, yo, p5, k2; rep from * to end.

Row 7 P2, *k6, yo, k3, ssk, k3, p2; rep from * to end.

Row 8 K2, *p2, p2tog tbl, p3, yo, p7, k2; rep from * to end.

Row 9 P2, *k8, yo, k3, ssk, k1, p2; rep from * to end.

Row 10 K2, *p2tog tbl, p3, yo, p9, k2; rep from * to end.

Rep rows 1–10.

190 diagonal crossed knots

(multiple of 4 sts)

LT (left twist) Sl 1 to cn and hold to *front*, k1, k1, from cn.

Row 1 (RS) *K2, p2; rep from * to end.

Rows 2 and 4 *K2, p2; rep from * to end.

Row 3 *LT, p2; rep from * to end.

Rows 5, 6 and 8 *P2, k2; rep from * to end.

Row 7 * P2, LT; rep from * to end.

Rep rows 1–8.

This pattern can also be knitted in reverse direction:

RT (right twist) Sl 1 to cn and hold to *back*, k1, k1 from cn.

Row 1 (RS) *P2, k2; rep from * to end.

Rows 2 and 4 *P2, k2; rep from * to end.

Row 3 *P2, RT; rep from * to end.

Rows 5, 6 and 8 *K2, p2; rep from * to end.

Row 7 *RT, p2; rep from * to end.

Rep rows 1–8.

traveling

189

190

191 diagonal eyelet mosaic

(multiple of 16 sts plus 2)

Row 1 (RS) K1, *K2, yo, ssk, k4, yo, ssk, k3, k2tog, yo, k1; rep from * end k1.

Row 2 and all WS rows K1, purl to last st, k1.

Row 3 K1, *K3, yo, ssk, k4, yo, ssk, k1, k2tog, yo, k2; rep from *, end k1.

Row 5 K1, *k4, yo, ssk, k4, yo, k3tog, yo, k3; rep from * to end, k1.

Row 7 K1, *k5, yo, ssk, k4, yo, ssk, k3; rep from * to end, k1.

Row 9 K1, *k3, k2tog, yo, k1, yo, ssk, k4, yo, ssk, k2; rep from * to end, k1.

Row 11 K1, *k2, k2tog, yo, k3, yo, ssk, k4, yo, ssk, k1; rep from * to end, k1.

Row 13 K1, *k1, k2tog, yo, k5, yo, ssk, k4, yo, ssk; rep from * to end, k1.

Row 15 k1, *k3 tog, yo, k4, k2tog, yo, k1, yo, ssk, k4, yo; rep from * to end, k1.

Row 17 k1, * Yo, k4, k2tog, yo, k3, yo, ssk, k3, k2tog; rep from * to end, k1.

Row 19 K1, *k4, k2tog, yo, k5, yo, ssk, k1, k2tog, yo; rep from * to end, k1.

Row 21 K1, *k3, k2tog, yo, k7, yo, k3tog, yo, k1; rep from * to end, k1.

Row 23 K1, *k2, k2tog, yo, k8, k2tog, yo, k2; rep from * to end, k1.

Row 25 K1, *k1, k2tog, yo, k1, yo, ssk, k5, k2tog, yo, k3; rep from * to end, k1.

Row 27 K1, *k2 tog, yo, k3, yo, ssk, k3, k2tog, yo, k4; rep from * to end, k1.

Row 29 K1, *yo, k5, yo, ssk, k1, k2tog, yo, k4, k2tog; rep from * to end, k1.

Row 31 K1,*k1, yo, ssk, k4, yo, k3tog, yo, k4, k2tog, yo; rep from * to end, k1.

Row 32 K1, purl to last st, k1.

Rep rows 1–32.

191

(multiple of 15 sts plus 5)

Row 1 (RS) K2, *k3, [yo, ssk] 3 times, [k2tog, yo] 3 times; rep from *, end k3.

Row 2 and all WS rows Purl.

Row 3 K2, *k4, [yo, ssk] 3 times, [k2tog, yo] twice, k1; rep from *, end k3.

Row 5 K2, *k5, [yo, ssk] 3 times, k2tog, yo, k2; rep from *, end k3.

Row 7 K2, *k6, [yo, ssk] 3 times, k3; rep from *, end k3.

Row 9 K2, *k4, k2tog, yo, k1, [yo, ssk] 3 times, k2; rep from *, end k3.

Row 11 K2, *k3, [k2tog, yo] twice, k1, [yo, ssk] 3 times, k1; rep from *, end k3.

Row 13 K2, *k2, [k2tog, yo] 3 times, k1, [yo, ssk] 3 times; rep from *, end k3.

Row 15 K1, yo, *ssk, [k2tog, yo] 3 times, k3, [yo, ssk] twice, yo; rep from *, end ssk, k2.

Row 17 K2, *[k2tog, yo] 3 times, k5, [yo, ssk] twice; rep from *, end k3.

Row 19 K1, *[k2tog, yo] 3 times, k7, yo, ssk; rep from *, end k2tog, yo, k2.

Row 21 K2, *[k2tog, yo] twice, k9, k2tog, yo; rep from *, end k2tog, yo, k1.

Row 23 K1, k2tog, *yo, k2tog, yo, k1, yo, ssk, k6, k2tog, yo, k2tog; rep from *, end yo, k2.

Row 25 K2, k2tog, yo, *k1, [yo, ssk] twice, k4, [k2tog, yo] 3 times; rep from *, end k1.

Row 27 K1, k2tog, yo, *k1, [yo, ssk] 3 times, k2, [k2tog, yo] 3 times; rep from *, end k2.

Row 28 Purl.

Rep rows 1–28.

193 eyelet links

(worked over 25 sts)

Row 1 (RS) K5, k2tog, yo, k6, k2tog, yo, k1 tbl, yo, ssk, k7.

Row 2 and all WS rows Purl.

Row 3 K4, k2tog, yo, k6, k2tog, yo, k3, yo, ssk, k6.

Row 5 K3, k2tog, yo, k6, k2tog, yo, k5, yo, ssk, k5.

Row 7 K2, k2tog, yo, k1 tbl, yo, ssk, k3, k2tog, yo, k1 tbl, yo, ssk, k4, yo, ssk, k4.

Row 9 K1, k2tog, yo, k3, yo, ssk, k1, k2tog, yo, k3, yo, ssk, k4, yo, ssk, k3.

Row 11 K2tog, yo, k5, yo, SK2P, yo, k1 tbl, yo, SK2P, yo, k1 tbl, yo, ssk, k4, yo, ssk, k2.

Row 13 K2, yo, ssk, k4, yo, ssk, k6, yo, ssk, k4, yo, ssk, k1.

Row 15 K3, yo, ssk, k4, yo, ssk, yo, k3tog, yo, k2tog, yo, k1 tbl, yo, ssk, k4, yo, ssk.

Row 17 K4, yo, ssk, k7, k2tog, yo, k3, yo, ssk, k1, k2tog, yo, k2.

Row 19 K5, yo, ssk, k4, yo, k3tog, yo, k5, yo, k3tog, yo, k3.

Row 21 K6, yo, ssk, k3, k2tog, yo, k6, k2tog, yo, k4.

Row 23 K7, yo, ssk, k1, k2tog, yo, k6, k2tog, yo, k5.

Row 25 K8, yo, k3tog, yo, k6, k2tog, yo, k6.

Row 27 K8, k2tog, yo, k6, k2tog, yo, k7.

Row 29 K7, k2tog, yo, k6, k2tog, yo, k8.

Row 31 K6, k2tog, yo, k6, k2tog, yo, k9.

Row 32 Purl.

Rep rows 1–32.

193

194 eyelet and flame chevron

(multiple of 7 sts plus 8)

Row 1 (RS) K5, *ssk, k5, yo; rep from *, end k3.

Row 2 and all WS rows Purl.

Row 3 K5, *ssk, k4, yo, k1; rep from *, end k3.

Row 5 K5, *ssk, k3, yo, k2; rep from *, end k3.

Row 7 K5, *ssk, k2, yo, k3; rep from *, end k3.

Row 9 K5, *ssk, k1, yo, k4; rep from *, end k3.

Row 11 K5, *ssk, yo, k5; rep from *, end k3.

Row 13 K3, *yo, k5, k2tog; rep from *, end k5.

Row 15 K3, *k1, yo, k4, k2tog; rep from *, end k5.

Row 17 K3, *k2, yo, k3, k2tog; rep from *, end k5.

Row 19 K3, *k3, yo, k2, k2tog; rep from *, end k5.

Row 21 K3, *k4, yo, k1, k2tog; rep from *, end k5.

Row 23 K3, *k5, yo, k2tog; rep from *, end k5.

Row 24 Purl.

Rep rows 1–24 .

195 meandering eyelet vines

(multiple of 12 sts plus 4)

Row 1 (RS) Knit.

Row 2 and all WS rows Purl.

Rows 3, 5, 7, 9 and 11 K1, *k2, ssk, k2tog, k4, [yo, k1] twice; rep from *,

end k3.

Row 13 Knit.

Rows 15, 17, 19, 21 and 23 K1, *k3, yo, k1, yo, k4, ssk, k2tog; rep from *, end k3.

Row 24 Purl.

Rep rows 1–24.

traveling

194

195

196 eyelet swirls

(multiple of 10 sts plus 2)

Row 1 (RS) K1, *yo, k8, k2tog; rep from *, end k1.
Row 2 P1, *p2tog, p7, yo, p1; rep from *, end p1.
Row 3 K1, *k2, yo, k6, k2tog; rep from *, end k1.
Row 4 P1, *p2tog, p5, yo, p3; rep from *, end p1.
Row 5 K1, *k4, yo, k4, k2tog; rep from *, end k1.
Row 6 P1, *p2tog, p3, yo, p5; rep from *, end p1.
Row 7 K1, *k6, yo, k2, k2tog; rep from *, end k1.
Row 8 P1, *p2tog, p1, yo, p7; rep from *, end p1.
Row 9 K1, *k8, yo, k2tog; rep from *, end k1.
Row 10 P1, *yo, p8, p2tog tbl; rep from *, end p1.
Row 11 K1, *ssk, k7, yo, k1; rep from *, end k1.
Row 12 P1, *p2, yo, p6, p2tog tbl; rep from *, end p1.
Row 13 K1, *ssk, k5, yo, k3; rep from * to last st, end k1.
Row 14 P1, *p4, yo, p4, p2tog tbl; rep from *, end p1.
Row 15 K1, *ssk, k3, yo, k5; rep from *, end k1.
Row 16 P1, *p6, yo, p2, p2tog tbl; rep from *, end p1.
Row 17 K1, *ssk, k1, yo, k7; rep from *, end k1.
Row 18 P1, *p8, yo, p2tog tbl; rep from *, end p1.
Rep rows 1–18.

196

197 twisted vine eyelet

(multiple of 10 sts plus 2)

Preparation row K1, p to last st, k1.

Row 1 (RS) K1, *yo, ssk, k8; rep from *, end k1.

Rows 2 and 12 K1, *yo, p2tog, p5, p2tog tbl, yo, p1; rep from *, end k1.

Rows 3 and 13 K1, *k2, yo, ssk, k3, k2tog, yo, k1; rep from *, end k1.

Rows 4 and 14 K1, *p2, yo, p2tog, p1, p2tog tbl, yo, p3; rep from *, end k1.

Row 5 K1, *k4, yo, k3tog, yo, k3; rep from *, end k1.

Row 6 K1, *[p3, p2tog tbl, yo] twice; rep from *, end k1.

Row 7 K1, *[k1, yo, ssk, k2] twice; rep from *, end k1.

Row 8 K1, *[p1, p2tog tbl, yo, p2] twice; rep from *, end k1.

Row 9 K1, *[k3, yo, ssk] twice; rep from *, end k1.

Row 10 K1, * [yo, p3, p2tog tbl] twice; rep from *, end k1.

Row 11 K1, * [yo, ssk, k3] twice; rep from *, end k1.

Rows 15 and 25 K1, *k4, yo, k3tog, yo, k3; rep from *, end k1.

Row 16 K1, *[p2tog, p3, yo] twice; rep from *, end k1.

Row 17 K1, *[k3, k2tog, yo] twice; rep from *, end k1.

Row 18 K1, *[p1, yo, p2tog, p2] twice; rep from *, end k1.

Row 19 K1, *[k1, k2tog, yo, k2] twice; rep from *, end k1.

Row 20 K1, *[p3, yo, p2tog] twice; rep from *, end k1.

Row 21 K1, *[yo, k3, k2tog] twice; rep from *, end k1.

Row 22 K1, *yo, p2tog, p5, p2tog tbl, yo, p1; rep from *, end k1.

Row 23 K1, *k2, yo, ssk, k3, k2tog, yo, k1; rep from *, end k1.

Row 24 K1, *p2, yo, p2tog, p1, p2tog tbl, yo, p3; rep from *, end k1.

Row 26 K1, p to last st, k1.

Rep rows 1–26.

197

198 eyelet leaves

(worked over 20 sts)

S2KP sl 2 knitwise, k1, pass 2 slipped sts over k1.

Row 1 (RS) P2, k9, yo, k1, yo, k3, SK2P, p2.

Row 2 and all WS rows K2, p16, k2.

Row 3 P2, k10, yo, k1, yo, k2, SK2P, p2.

Row 5 P2, k3tog, k4, yo, k1, yo, k3, [yo, k1] twice, SK2P, p2.

Row 7 P2, k3tog, k3, yo, k1, yo, k9, p2.

Row 9 P2, k3tog, k2, yo, k1, yo, k10, p2.

Row 11 P2, k3tog, [k1, yo] twice, k3, yo, k1, yo, k4, SK2P, p2.

Row 12 K2, p16, k2.

Rep rows 1–12.

199 eyelet rib

(multiple of 4 sts plus 2)

Row 1 (RS) K2, *k2tog, yo, k2; rep from * to end.

Rows 2, 4, 6, 8, 10 and 12 Purl.

Row 3 K1, *k2tog, yo, k2; rep from *, end last rep k3.

Row 5 *K2tog, yo, k2; rep from *, end last rep k4.

Row 7 K1, *yo, ssk, k2; rep from *, end last rep k3.

Row 9 K2, *yo, ssk, k2; rep from * to end.

Row 11 K1, *k2, yo, ssk; rep from *, end k1.

Rows 13, 15, 17 and 19 K2, *p2, k2; rep from * to end.

Rows 14, 16, 18 and 20 P2, *k2, p2; rep from * to end.

Rep rows 1–20.

200 zigzag eyelets

(work over 17 sts)
Rows 1, 3, 5 and 7 (RS) P2, k2, yo, k2tog, ssk, [k2, yo] twice, k2tog, k1, p2.
Rows 2, 4, 6 and 8 K2, p2, yo, p2tog, p6, yo, p2tog, p1, k2.
Rows 9, 11, 13 and 15 P2, k2, yo, k2tog, k1, yo, k2, k2tog, k1, yo, k2tog, k1, p2.
Rows 10, 12, 14 and 16 K2, p2, yo, p2tog, p6, yo, p2tog, p1, k2.
Rep rows 1–16.

201 anemone

(multiple of 4 sts plus 2)
Rows 1–4 Knit.
Row 5 (RS) K1, *k1 wrapping yarn around needle twice; rep from *, end k1.
Row 6 K1, *sl 4 sts to RH needle, dropping extra wrap, sl sts back to LH needle, k same 4 sts tog without dropping from LH, p1, k1, p1 into same 4 sts, sl them off the needle; rep from *, end k1.
Rep rows 1–6.

traveling

200

201

202 embossed vine and leaves

(worked over 26 sts)

S2KP sl 2 knitwise, k1, pass 2 slipped sts over k1.

K inc (knit increase) knit into front and back of stitch.

P inc (purl increase) Purl into front and back of stitch

Row 1 (WS) K5, p5, k4, p3, k9.

Row 2 P7, p2tog, k inc, k2, p4, k2, yo, k1, yo, k2, p5 – 28 sts.

Row 3 K5, p7, k4, p2, k1, p1, k8.

Row 4 P6, p2tog, k1, p inc, k2, p4, k3, yo, k1, yo, k3, p5 – 30 sts.

Row 5 K5, p9, k4, p2, k2, p1, k7.

Row 6 P5, p2tog, k1, p inc, p1, k2, p4, ssk, k5, k2tog, p5 – 28 sts.

Row 7 K5, p7, k4, p2, k3, p1, k6.

Row 8 P4, p2tog, k1, p inc, p2, k2, p4, ssk, k3, k2tog, p5 – 26 sts.

Row 9 K5, p5, k4, p2, k4, p1, k5.

Row 10 P5, yo, k1, yo, p4, k2, p4, ssk, k1, k2tog, p5.

Row 11 K5, p3, k4, p2, k4, p3, k5.

Row 12 P5, [yo, k1] twice, k1, p4, k1, M1, k1, p2tog, p2, S2KP, p5.

Row 13 K9, p3, k4, p5, k5.

Row 14 P5, k2, yo, k1, yo, k2, p4, k1, k inc, k1, p2tog, p7 – 28 sts.

Row 15 K8, p1, k1, p2, k4, p7, k5.

Row 16 P5, k3, yo, k1, yo, k3, p4, k2, p inc, k1, p2tog, p6 – 30 sts.

Row 17 K7, p1, k2, p2, k4, p9, k5.

Row 18 P5, ssk, k5, k2tog, p4, k2, p1, p inc, k1, p2tog, p5 – 28 sts.

Row 19 K6, p1, k3, p2, k4, p7, k5.

Row 20 P5, ssk, k3, k2tog, p4, k2, p2, p inc, k1, p2tog, p4 – 26 sts.

Row 21 K5, p1, k4, p2, k4, p5, k5.

Row 22 P5, ssk, k1, k2tog, p4, k2, p4, yo, k1, yo, p5.

Row 23 K5, p3, k4, p2, k4, p3, k5.

Row 24 P5, S2KP, p2, p2tog, k1, M1, k1, p4, [yo, k1] twice, k1, p5.

Rep rows 1-24.

202

172 horizontal waves

(multiple of 14 sts plus 2)

Rows 1 and 3 (RS) K1, *[k1 tbl, p1] twice, k1 tbl, p2, k7; rep from *, end k1.

Rows 2 and 4 K1, *p7, k2, p1 tbl, [k1, p1 tbl] twice; rep from *, end k1.

Row 5 K1, *[k1 tbl, p1] 3 times, k2tog, k6, M1; rep from *, end k1.

Row 6 K1, *p1 tbl, p7, [k1, p1 tbl] 3 times; rep from *, end k1.

203

Row 7 K1, *[k1 tbl, p1] twice, k1 tbl, k2tog, k6, M1 p-st, k1 tbl; rep from *, end k1.

Row 8 K1, *p1 tbl, k1, p7, p1 tbl, [k1, p1 tbl] twice, rep from *, end k1.

Row 9 K1, *[k1 tbl, p1] twice, k2tog, k6, M1, p1, k1 tbl; rep from *, end k1.

Row 10 K1, *p1 tbl, k1, p1 tbl, p7, [k1, p1 tbl] twice; rep from *, end k1.

Row 11 K1, *k1 tbl, p1, k1 tbl, k2tog, k6, M1 p-st, k1 tbl, p1, k1 tbl; rep from *, end k1.

Row 12 K1, *[p1 tbl, k1] twice, p7, p1 tbl, k1, p1 tbl.

Row 13 K1, *k1 tbl, p1, k2tog, k6, M1, [p1, k1 tbl] twice.

Row 14 K1, *[p1 tbl, k1] twice, p1 tbl, p7, k1, p1 tbl.

Row 15 K1, *k1 tbl, k2tog, k6, M1 p-st, [k1 tbl, p1] twice, k1 tbl.

Row 16 K1, *[p1 tbl, k1] 3 times, p7, p1 tbl; rep from *, end k1.

Row 17 K1, *k2tog, k6, M1 p-st, [p1, k1 tbl] 3 times.

Row 18 K1, *[p1 tbl, k1] twice, p1 tbl, k2, p7; rep from *, end k1.

Row 19 K1, *k7, p2, k1 tbl, [p1, k1 tbl] twice; rep from *, end k1.

Row 20 K1, *[p1 tbl, k1] twice, p1 tbl, k2, p7; rep from *, end k1.

Row 21 K1, *k7, p2, k1 tbl, [p1, k1 tbl] twice; rep from *, end k1.

Row 22 K1, *[p1 tbl, k1] twice, p1 tbl, k2, p7; rep from *, end k1.

Row 23 K1, *M1, k6, ssk, [p1, k1 tbl] 3 times; rep from *, end k1.

Row 24 K1, *[p1 tbl, k1] 3 times, p7, p1 tbl; rep from *, end k1.

Row 25 K1, *k1 tbl, M1 p-st, k6, ssk, k1 tbl, [p1, k1 tbl] twice; rep from *, end k1.

Row 26 K1, *[p1 tbl, k1] twice, p1 tbl, p7, k1, p1 tbl; rep from *, end k1.

Row 27 K1, *k1 tbl, p1, M1, k6, ssk, [p1, k1 tbl] twice; rep from *, end k1.

Row 28 K1, *[p1 tbl, k1] twice, p7, p1 tbl, k1, p 1 tbl; rep from *, end k1.

Row 29 K1, *k1 tbl, p1, k1 tbl, M1 p-st, k6, ssk, k1 tbl, p1, k1 tbl; rep from *, end k1.

Row 30 K1, *p1 tbl, k1, p1 tbl, p7, [k1, p1 tbl] twice; rep from *, end k1.

Row 31 K1, *[k1 tbl, p1] twice, M1, k6, ssk, p1, k1 tbl; rep from *, end k1.

Row 32 K1, *p1 tbl, k1, p7, p1 tbl, [k1, p1 tbl] twice; rep from *, end k1.

Row 33 K1, *[k1 tbl, p1] twice, k1 tbl M1 p-st, k6, ssk, k1 tbl; rep from *, end k1.

Row 34 K1, *p1 tbl, p7, [k1, p1 tbl] 3 times.

Row 35 K1, *[k1 tbl, p1] 3 times, M1 p-st, k6, ssk; rep from *, end k1.

Row 36 K1, *p7, k2, p1 tbl, [k1, p1 tbl] twice.

Rep rows 1–36.

204 vines rib

(multiple of 15 sts)

RPT (right purl twist) Sl 1 st to cn and hold to *back*, k1, p1 from cn.

LPT (left purl twist) Sl 1 st to cn and hold to *front*, p1, k1 from cn.

Row 1 (RS) *K4 tbl, p4, k3 tbl, p4; rep from * to end.

Row 2 *K4, p3 tbl, k4, p4 tbl; rep from * to end.

Row 3 *K4 tbl, p3, RPT, k1 tbl, LPT, p3; rep from * to end.

Row 4 *K3, [p1 tbl, k1] 3 times, k2, p4 tbl; rep from * to end.

Row 5 *K4 tbl, p2, RPT, p1, k1 tbl, p1, LPT, p2; rep from * to end.

Row 6 *[K2, p1 tbl] 3 times, k2, p4 tbl; rep from * to end.

Row 7 *K4 tbl, p1, RPT, p2, k1 tbl, p2, LPT, p1; rep from * to end.

Row 8 *K1, [p1 tbl, k3] twice, p1 tbl, k1, p4 tbl; rep from * to end.

Row 9 *K4 tbl, RPT, p3, k1 tbl, p3, LPT; rep from * to end.

Row 10 *[P1 tbl, k4] twice, p5 tbl; rep from * to end.

Rep rows 1–10.

204

unusual

205 condo knitting

(worked over any number of sts)

Materials

Needle size on yarn label.

Size 35 (19mm) needles.

With smaller needles, cast on.

Row 1 (RS) With smaller needles, knit.

Row 2 With larger needles, knit.

Rep rows 1 and 2.

Work to desired length, end with RS row.

With smaller needles, bind off.

206 condo knitting stripes

(worked over any number of sts)

Materials

2 sets of needles, six sizes apart.

Cast on with smaller needles.

Rows 1–5 With smaller needles, [p 1 row, k 1 row] twice, p 1 row.

Row 6 (RS) With larger needles, *p next st wrapping yarn twice around needle; rep from * to end.

Row 7 With smaller needles, knit dropping extra wrapped st.

Rows 8–12 With smaller needles, [k 1 row, p 1 row] twice, k 1 row.

Row 13 With larger needles, *k next st wrapping yarn twice around needle; rep from * to end.

Row 14 With smaller needles, purl dropping extra wrapped st.

Rep rows 1–14.

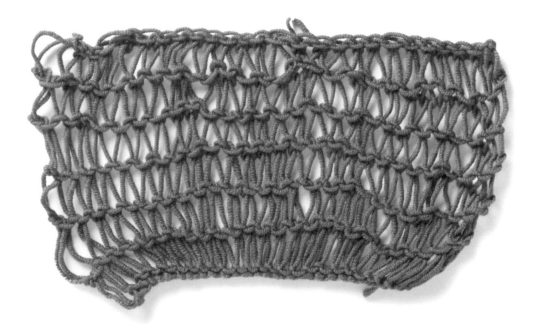

205

206

207 pucker stitch

(multiple of 34 sts plus 2)

MP (make pucker)
Wyif, insert needle from top into loop of next st 10 rows below, pick up this loop, place on LH needle and purl tog with next st on current row.

Row 1 (RS) Knit.
Row 2 Purl.
Rows 3-21 Work in St st.
Row 22 (WS) P1, *MP in next 17 sts, p17; rep from *, end p1.
Rows 23–41 Work in St st.
Row 42 P1, *p17, MP in next 17 sts; rep from *, end p1.
Rep rows 3–42.

208 double stockinette stitch

(worked over an odd number of sts)

Note This stitch creates a double-faced fabric
Row 1 (RS) K1, * wyib sl 1, k1; rep from *, to end.
Row 2 K1, *p1, k1; rep from * to end.
Rep rows 1 and 2.

207

208

209 seed stitch blocks

(multiple of 7 sts plus 5)
Rows 1, 3 and 5 (RS) *[K1, p1] twice, k1, k2; rep from *, end [k1, p1] twice, k1.
Rows 2, 4 and 6 *[K1, p1] twice, k1, p2; rep from *, end [k1, p1] twice, k1.
Row 7 Purl.
Row 8 Knit.
Rep rows 1–8.

210 puckered stripes

(worked over any number of sts)
Materials
Small and large needles (ie: sizes 5 and 8)
Two contrasting weight yarns (Yarn A = worsted weight / Yarn B = super fine weight)
Row 1 (RS) With larger needles and B, *k into front and back of next st; rep from * to end. There are double the amount of sts from previous row.
Rows 2–8 With larger needles and B, work in St st.
Row 9 With smaller needles and A, *k2tog; rep from * to end. There are half the number of sts from previous row.
Row 10–14 With smaller needles and A, knit.
Rep rows 1–14.

209

210

211 ladder and rib

(multiple of 12 sts plus 3)

DL (drop ladder)

Sl next st from LH needle and let it unravel for 7 rows.

Row 1 (RS) P3, *k3, p3, k3, p3; rep from * to end.

Row 2 K3, *p3, k3, p3, k3; rep from * to end.

Row 3 P3, *k3, p3, k2, M1, k1, p3; rep from * to end.

Rows 4, 6, 8 and 10 K3, *p4, k3, p3, k3; rep from * to end.

Rows 5, 7 and 9 P3, *k3, p3, k4, p3; rep from * to end.

Row 11 P3, *k2, M1, k1, p3, k2, DL, k1, p3; rep from * to end.

Rows 12, 14, 16 and 18 K3, *p3, k3, p4, k3; rep from * to end.

Rows 13, 15 and 17 P3, *k4, p3, k3, p3; rep from * to end.

Row 19 P3, *k2, DL, k1, p3, k2, M1, k1, p3; rep from * to end.

Row 20 K3, *p4, k3, p3, k3; rep from * to end.

Rep rows 5–20.

212 long stitch tile

(multiple of 6 sts plus 2)

LS (long st) With RH needle in front of work, pick up next st 6 rows below and place on LH needle, then k this st tog with next st on LH needle pulling up long loop.

Rows 1–6 Work in St st (k 1 row, p 1 row).

Row 7 (RS) K1, *k3, LS, k2; rep from *, end k1.

Row 8 Purl.

Rows 9–14 Work in St st.

Row 15 K7, *LS, k5; rep from *, end k1.

Row 16 Purl.

Rep rows 1–16.

unusual

211

212

213 fancy garter ridges

(worked over an even number of sts)

Row 1 (RS) Knit.

Row 2 *K2tog; rep from * to end.

Row 3 K into front and back of each st across row.

Rows 4 and 6 Purl.

Rows 5 and 7 Knit.

Row 8 Rep row 2.

Row 9 Rep row 3.

Row 10 Purl.

Rep rows 1–10.

214 smocked ribbing

(multiple of 4 sts plus 1)

Materials

Yarn needle

Contrasting yarn

Row 1 (RS) *K1, p3; rep from *, end k1.

Row 2 *P1, k3; rep from *, end p1.

Rep rows 1 and 2 for smocked ribbing.

Smocking

Mark smocking rows by basting contrasting yarn under the knit sts in row 6, row 14 and every following 8th row. Thread main yarn through needle and hold needle to WS of work.

Beginning at 2nd knit st of first marked row, bring needle up RH side of st and through work to RS, *insert needle under first marked st, then under 2nd, bring needle through and pull to join knit sts; rep from * once more (smock st). From WS of work, bring needle up LH side of next marked row and work smock st to join 2nd and 3rd knit sts, bring needle up RH side of next marked row and work smock st to join 1st and 2nd sts. Cont to alternate smock sts to top and across work.

213

214

215 smocked stockinette

(worked over a background of St st)

With a contrasting yarn or sewing thread, mark the sts and rows you want to smock. For example: every 6 sts and every 6 rows. With RS facing and main yarn, work smock sts as for smocked ribbing. See page 146.

216 ric rac and garter

(multiple of 6 sts)

RPT (right purl twist) Wyif skip first st, p second st, then p skipped st,

sl both sts from needle.

LT (left twist) With RH needle behind LH needle, skip next st on LH

needle, k second st tbl, then k skipped st in front loop, sl both sts from LH needle.

Row 1 (RS) K2, *LT, k4; rep from *, end LT, k2.

Row 2 K2, *RPT, k4; rep from *, end RPT, k2.

Rep rows 1 and 2.

unusual

215

216

217 tiny herringbone

(multiple of 4 sts plus 2)

RT (right twist) Skip 1 st and k the 2nd st, knit skipped st and sl both sts from needle tog.

LT (left twist) Skip 1 st passing behind this st, k the 2nd st tbl, knit the skipped st in front loop and sl both sts from needle tog.

Row 1 (RS) K to last st, sl 1.

Row 2 P to last st, sl 1.

Row 3 K1, *RT, LT; rep from *, end sl 1.

Row 4 Rep row 2.

Rep rows 3 and 4.

218 tiny herringbone eyelet

(multiple of 4 sts plus 3)

RT (right twist) Skip 1 st and k the 2nd st, knit skipped st and sl both sts from needle tog.

LT (left twist) Skip 1 st passing behind this st, k the 2nd st tbl, knit the skipped st in front loop and sl both sts from needle tog.

Cast on a multiple of 4 sts plus 2.

Row 1 (RS) K1, *yo, k4; rep from *, end sl 1.

Rows 2 and 4 P to last st, sl 1.

Row 3 K1, *yo, k the 3rd st leaving all 3 sts on LH needle, k the first st and the 2nd st tog and sl from needle, LT; rep from *, end sl 1.

Rep rows 3 and 4.

217

218

219 twisted waffle

(multiple of 4 sts plus 2)

Note Bind off in the pattern of the new row as you work it.

Rows 1 and 3 (RS) *K2, skip the next st and knit the second passing in back of first, then knit the first and let both fall from the needle; rep from *, end k2.

Row 2 Purl.

Row 4 *K2, p2; rep from *, end k2.

Repeat rows 1–4.

220 linen stitch

(worked over an even number of sts)

Row 1 (RS) *K1, wyif sl 1; rep from * to end.

Row 2 *P1, wyib sl 1; rep from * to end.

Rep rows 1 and 2.

219

220

221 snakeskin

(multiple of 2 sts plus 1)
Row 1 (RS) *K2, wyif sl 2 sts, bring yarn to back, return 2 sl sts to LH needle and k2;
rep from *, end k3.
Rows 2 and 4 Purl.
Row 3 K4, *wyif sl 2 sts, bring yarn to back, return 2 sl sts to LH needle and k2, k2;
rep from *, end k1.
Repeat rows 1–4.

222 tiny scales

(multiple of 4 sts plus 2)
Rows 1 and 3 (WS) Purl.
Row 2 K1, *insert RH needle from behind under running thread between st just
worked and next st, thus putting an extra strand on the needle, k next 2 sts, then
with LH needle pass extra strand over 2 k sts, k2; rep from *, end k1.
Row 4 K3; rep from * of row 2, end last rep k1.
Rep rows 1–4.

221

222

223 schiaparelli pattern

(worked over an even number of sts)

Crossed stitch Insert RH needle through the front loop of the first st and then k the second st through front loop in one motion from this position, then k the first st still on the needle tbl and slip both sts from needle tog.

Row 1 (RS) *Work crossed st over next 2 sts; rep from * to end.

Rows 2 and 4 Purl.

Row 3 K1, *work crossed st over next 2 sts; rep from *, end k1.

Rep rows 1–4.

224 tiny bamboo

(multiple of 2 sts)

Note Bind off purlwise across row 2.

Row 1 (RS) *Yo, k2, pass the yo over the k2; rep from * to end.

Row 2 Purl.

Repeat rows 1 and 2.

unusual

223

224

225 woven rattan

(over an odd number of sts)

Row 1 (WS) *P2tog and leave sts on needle, p first st again, drop both sts tog from LH needle; rep from *, end k1.

Row 2 *Wyib sl 1, k1, with tip of LH needle raise up sl st slightly, pull RH needle through raised st as for a psso but do not drop raised st from LH needle, k1 tbl of raised st and drop from needle; rep from *, end k1.

Rep rows 1 and 2.

226 woven slip stitch

(multiple of 3 sts plus 2)

3-st RC (3 stitch right cross)

Sl 2 sts to cn and hold to *back*, k1, (k1, sl 1) from cn.

3-st LC (3 stitch left cross)

Sl 1 st to cn and hold to *front*, sl 1, k1, then k1 from cn.

Rows 1 and 3 (RS) K1, *k2, wyib sl 1; rep from *, end k1.

Rows 2 and 4 K1, *wyif sl 1, p2; rep from *, end k1.

Row 5 K1, *3-st RC; rep from *, end k1.

Rows 6 and 8 K1, p3, *wyif sl 1, p2; rep from *, end k1.

Row 7 K1, *k2, wyib sl 1; rep from *, end k4.

Row 9 K1, k2, *3-st LC; rep from *, end wyib sl 1, k1.

Rep rows 2–9.

225

226

227 brioche honeycomb

(worked over an even number of sts)

K1-b (knit 1 in row below)

Rows 1 and 2 Knit.

Row 3 (RS) *K1, k1-b (this will form a loose strand at back of st); rep from * to end.

Row 4 *Insert RH needle under loose strand of next st and in st, k strand and st tog, k1; rep from * to end.

Row 5 *K1-b, k1; rep from * to end.

Row 6 *K1, k loose strand and next st tog; rep from * to end.

Rep rows 3–6.

228 smocking stitch

(multiple of 6 sts plus 3)

Row 1 (WS) K1, p1, *wyib sl 5 sts, p1; rep from *, end k1.

Row 2 Knit.

Row 3 K1, p across to last st, k1.

Row 4 K1, wyib sl 3, *insert needle under loose strand of row 1 and k tog with next st, bringing yarn out from under stand so strand is caught behind st, wyib sl 5; rep from *, end last rep wyib sl 3, k1.

Row 5 K1, wyib sl 3, p1, *wyib sl 5, p1; rep from *, end wyib sl 3, k1.

Rows 6 and 7 Rep rows 2 and 3.

Row 8 K1, *k loose strand and next st tog as established, wyib sl 5; rep from *, end k loose strand and next st tog, k1.

Rep rows 1–8.

unusual

227

228

229 bubble stitch

(multiple of 6 sts plus 3)

Row 1 (RS) Knit.

Rows 2 and 4 *Wyif sl 3 sts, p3; rep from *, end wyif sl 3 sts.

Row 3 *Wyib sl 3 sts, k3; rep from *, end wyib sl 3 sts.

Rows 5 and 7 Knit.

Row 6 Purl.

Row 8 K1, *insert needle from below under the 3 loose strands of rows 2, 3 and 4 and k next st, bringing st out under strands, p5; rep from *, end last rep k1.

Row 9 Knit.

Rows 10 and 12 *P3, wyif sl 3 sts; rep from *, end p3.

Row 11 K3, *wyib sl 3, k3; rep from * to end.

Rows 13 and 15 Knit.

Row 14 Purl.

Row 16 P4, *k next st through 3 loose strands of rows 10, 11 and 12, p5; rep from *, end p4 .

Rep rows 1–16.

230 butterfly stitch

(multiple of 10 sts plus 9)

Note On rows 10 and 20, work butterfly stitch loosely.

Rows 1, 3, 5, 7 and 9 (RS) K2, *wyif sl 5, k5; rep from *, end wyif sl 5, k2.

Rows 2, 4, 6 and 8 Purl.

Row 10 P4, *insert LH needle down through the 5 loose strands below next st, p these 5 strands tog with next st on needle, p9; rep from *, end last rep p4.

Rows 11, 13, 15, 17 and 19 K7, *wyif sl 5, k5; rep from *, end wyif sl 5, k7.

Rows 12, 14, 16 and 18 Purl.

Row 20 P9, *insert LH needle down through the 5 loose strands below next st, p these 5 strands tog with next st on needle, p9; rep from * to end.

Rep rows 1–20.

229

230

231 tassel stitch

(multiple of 6 sts plus 1)

Rows 1 and 3 (RS) *K4, p2; rep from *, end k1.

Rows 2 and 4 P1, *k2, p4; rep from * to end.

Row 5 *Put RH needle between 4th and 5th sts and bring through a loop making a st on RH needle, k1, p2, k3; rep from *, end k1.

Row 6 P1, *p3, k2, k2tog (regular st and st from loop made on previous row); rep from * to end.

Rows 7 and 9 K1, *p2, k4; rep from * to end.

Rows 8 and 10 *P4, k2; rep from *, end p1.

Row 11 K1, *k2, draw loop from between 4th and 5th sts onto RH needle, k1, p2, k1; rep from * to end.

Row 12 *P1, k2, p2tog, p2; rep from *, end p1.

Rep rows 1–12.

232 peruvian lace

(multiple of 4 sts plus 2)

Row 1 (RS) Knit.

Row 2 Knit.

Row 3 K1, *insert RH needle into next st, wrapping yarn around needle twice (double yo), complete knit st; rep from *, end k1.

Row 4 K1, *wyib sl 4 purlwise, dropping extra yo, sl these 4 sts back to LH needle, insert RH needle through all 4 sts, then k1, p1, k1, p1 into all 4 sts held tog, sl sts from LH needle; rep from *, end k1.

Rows 5, 6, 7 and 8 Knit.

Row 9 Rep row 3.

Row 10 Knit, dropping extra yo's.

Rep rows 1–10.

unusual

231

232

233 indian cross stitch

(multiple of 6 sts plus 2)

Row 1 (RS) Knit.

Row 2 K1, *yo twice, p1; rep from *, end k1.

Row 3 K1, *sl next 6 sts to RH needle, dropping extra yo's between sts. Sl these sts back to LH needle. Insert RH needle in 4th st, then lift it passing it over first, 2nd and 3rd sts. Sl 4th st back to LH needle, then k it. Working in this same manner, pass and k the 5th, then 6th st. Now k the first, 2nd and 3rd sts in that order; rep from *, end k1.

Row 4 K1, p to last st, end k1.

Row 5 Knit.

Row 6 K1, p1, *yo twice, p1; rep from *, end k1.

Row 7 K1, sl next 3 sts to RH needle, dropping extra yo's. Sl these 3 sts back to LH needle, then k the 3 sts, sl next 6 sts to RH needle, dropping extra yo's. Sl these sts back to LH needle as foll: insert LH needle into 3rd, 2nd then first st on RH needle, then lift them, passing them over the 4th, 5th and 6th sts onto LH needle. Sl the 6th, 5th and 4th sts back to LH needle in that order, then k the 6 sts; rep from *, end sl next 3 sts to RH needle, dropping extra yo's. Sl these 3 sts back to LH needle, then k the 3 sts, k1.

Row 8 Rep row 4.

Rep rows 1–8.

233

234 peacocks

(multiple of 8 sts plus 2)

RT (right twist) Skip next st and k second st in front of first st, then k first st, drop both sts from LH needle.

LT (left twist) Skip next st and k second st behind first st, then k first st, drop both sts from LH needle.

ES (elongated stitch) Insert RH needle into space between RT and LT four rows below where marker was placed, wrap yarn around needle and pull up a long loop.

Row 1 (RS) K4, *RT, k6; rep from *, end k4.

Rows 2, 4 and 6 Purl.

Row 3 K3, *RT, pm, LT, k4; rep from *, end k3.

Row 5 K2, *RT, k2, LT, k2; rep from * to end.

Row 7 K1, *k2tog, M1, [k1, ES] 4 times, M1, ssk; rep from *, end k1.

Row 8 P3, *[p2tog] 4 times, p4; rep from *, end p3.

Row 9 K5, *k3, RT, k3; rep from *, end k8.

Rows 10, 12 and 14 Purl.

Row 11 K5, *k2, RT, pm, LT, k2; rep from *, end k7.

Row 13 K5, *k1, RT, k2, LT, k1; rep from *, end k6.

Row 15 K5, *k2tog, M1, [k1, ES] 4 times, M1, ssk; rep from *, end k5.

Row 16 P5, *p2, [p2tog] 4 times, p2; rep from *, end p7.

Rep rows 1–16.

234

235 bluebells

(multiple of 6 sts plus 3)
Row 1 (RS) *Yo, SK2P, yo, p3; rep from *, end yo, SK2P, yo.
Row 2 Knit.
Rows 3 and 5 *K3, p3; rep from *, end k3.
Rows 4 and 6 P3, *k3, p3; rep from * to end.
Rep rows 1–6.

236 big bobbles

(multiple of 6 sts plus 2)
Row 1 (RS) P2, *k in front, back, front and back of next st (4 sts made in 1 st), p2, k1, p2; rep from * to end.
Rows 2 and 4 *K2, p1, k2, [k next st wrapping yarn twice around needle] 4 times; rep from *, end k2.
Rows 3 and 5 P2, *[k next stitch dropping extra yo] 4 times, p2, k1, p2; rep from * to end.
Row 6 *K2, p1, k2, p4tog; rep from *, end k2.
Row 7 P2, *k1, p2, k in front, back, front and back of next st (4 sts made in 1 st), p2; rep from * to end.
Rows 8 and 10 *K2, [k next st wrapping yarn twice around needle] 4 times, k2, p1; rep from *, end k2.
Rows 9 and 11 P2, *k1, p2, [k next stitch dropping extra yo] 4 times, p2; rep from * to end.
Row 12 *K2, p4tog, k2, p1; rep from *, end k2.
Rep rows 1–12.

235

236

237 zig zag

(multiple of 9 sts)

RT (right twist) Skip next st and k second st in front of first st, then k first st, drop both sts from LH needle.

LT (left twist) Skip next st and k second st behind first st, then k first st, drop both sts from LH needle.

Row 1 (RS) *LT 3 times, k3; rep from * to end.

Row 2 and all WS rows Purl.

Row 3 *K1, LT 3 times, k2; rep from * to end.

Row 5 *K2, LT 3 times, k1; rep from * to end.

Row 7 *K3, LT 3 times; rep from * to end.

Row 9 *K3, RT 3 times; rep from * to end.

Row 11 *K2, RT 3 times, k1; rep from * to end.

Row 13 *K1, RT 3 times, k2; rep from * to end.

Row 15 *RT 3 times, k3; rep from * to end.

Row 16 Purl.

Rep rows 1–16.

237

238 twist stitch diamonds

(multiple of 10 sts plus 2)

LT (left twist) With RH needle behind LH needle, sk first st and k the 2nd st in the back lp, then insert RH needle into the backs of both sts (the skipped st and the 2nd st) and k2tog tbl.

RT (right twist) K2tog, leaving sts on LH needle, then insert RH needle from the front between the two sts just knitted tog and k the first st again, then sl both sts from needle tog.

Row 1 (RS) K1, LT to last st, k1.

Rows 2 and all WS rows Purl.

Row 3 *RT, [LT] 4 times; rep from *, end RT.

Row 5 K1, *RT, [LT] 3 times, RT; rep from *, end k1.

Row 7 *[RT] twice, [LT] twice, RT; rep from *, end RT.

Row 9 K1, *[RT] twice, LT, [RT] twice; rep from *, end k1.

Row 11 Rep row 7.

Row 13 K1, *[RT] 3 times, LT, RT; rep from *, end k1.

Row 15 *[RT] 3 times, [LT] twice; rep from *, end RT.

Row 17 K1, *[RT] twice, [LT] 3 times; rep from *, end k1.

Row 19 *[RT] twice, [LT] 3 times; rep from *, end RT.

Row 20 Purl.

Rep rows 1–20.

238

239 tiny knots

(multiple of 10 sts plus 2)

MK (make knot) Wyif, p3tog leaving these sts on LH needle, then wyib, k the same 3 sts tog, then wyif p3tog again, sl sts from LH needle.

Rows 1 and 3 (RS) Knit.

Rows 2 and 4 Purl.

Row 5 *K7, MK; rep from *, end k2.

Rows 6, 8, 10, 12 and 14 Purl.

Rows 7, 9, 11 and 13 Knit.

Row 15 *K2, MK, k5; rep from *, end k2.

Rows 16 and 18 Purl.

Rows 17 and 19 Knit.

Row 20 Purl.

Rep rows 1–20.

240 stockinette dots

(multiple of 6 sts plus 1)

MK (make knot) Insert RH needle under running st between next 2 sts on LH needle, wrap yarn and loosely draw up a loop. Insert RH needle above same running thread and loosely draw up second loop. Wyif, p first st from LH needle. Pass first loop over 2nd loop and p st, then pass second loop over p st.

Rows 1 and 3 (WS) Purl.

Row 2 Knit.

Row 4 K3, *MK, k5; rep from *, end k3.

Rows 5 – 7 Rep rows 1 – 3.

Row 8 K6, *MK, k5; rep from *, end k1.

Rep rows 1–8.

239

240

241 bobble and rib

(multiple of 4 sts plus 1)

MB (make bobble) [P1, yo] twice, p1 in next st, turn, k5, turn, p5, turn, ssk, k1, k2tog, turn, p3tog.

Row 1 (RS) K2, p1, k1, *MB, k1, p1, k1; rep from *, end k1.

Row 2 K1, *p1, k1; rep from * to end.

Row 3 K2, *p1, k1; rep from *, end k1.

Rep rows 2 and 3.

242 blackberry stitch

(multiple of 4 sts)

Inc 2

K1, p1, k1 in one st.

Rows 1 and 3 (RS) Purl.

Row 2 *P3tog, inc 2; rep from * to end.

Row 4 *Inc 2, p3tog; rep from * to end.

Rep rows 1–4.

241

242

243 daisy chain

(multiple of 6 sts plus 1)

triple yo Insert RH needle into next st, wrapping yarn around needle 3 times, complete knit st.

cluster st Wyif, [sl next st, dropping extra 2 yo's] 5 times, [bring yarn to back between needles, sl 5 sts back to LH needle, bring yarn to front between needles, sl 5 sts to RH needle] twice.

Row 1 (RS) K1, *[triple yo] 5 times, k1; rep from * to end.

Row 2 K1, *cluster st, k1; rep from * to end.

Row 3 Knit (including each st of cluster st).

Rows 4, 5 and 7 Knit.

Rows 6 and 8 Purl.

Rows 9 and 10 Knit.

Row 11 K4*, [triple yo] 5 times, k1; rep from *, end k3.

Row 12 K4, *work cluster st over 5 sts, k1; rep from *, end k3.

Rows 13, 14, 15 and 17 Knit.

Rows 16 and 18 Purl.

Rows 19 and 20 Knit.

Rep rows 1–20.

243

244 boxed berries

(multiple of 6 sts plus 1)

k3tog (knit 3 sts together)

dec 4 (decrease 4) K2tog tbl, k3tog, sl k2tog st over k3tog st – 1 st rem.

Row 1 (RS) P3, *k1, p5; rep from *, end k1, p3.

Row 2 K3tog, *yo, [k1, yo, k1] in next st, yo, dec 4; rep from *, yo, [k1, p1, k1] in next st, yo, k3tog tbl.

Row 3 K1 tbl, *p5, k1tbl; rep from * to end.

Row 4 P1, *k5, p1; rep from * to end.

Row 5 K1, *p5, k1; rep from * to end.

Row 6 Purl into front and back of first st, yo, *dec 4, yo, [k1, yo, k1] in next st, yo; rep from *, end dec 4, yo, p into front and back of next st.

Row 7 P3, *k1 tbl, p5; rep from *, end k1 tbl, p3.

Row 8 K3, *p1, k5; rep from *, end p1, k3.

Rep rows 1–8.

245 lamb's tail

(multiple of 4 sts)

MB (make bobble) Cast on 3 sts on LH needle, bind off all 3 sts.

Row 1 (RS) *K3, MB; rep from * to end.

Rows 2 and 4 (WS) Purl.

Row 3 Knit.

Row 5 *K1, MB, k2; rep from * to end.

Rows 6–8 Rep rows 2–4.

Rep rows 1–8.

244

245

246 bobbles all over

(multiple of 6 sts plus 2)

MB (make bobble) [K1, p1, k1] in next st, turn, p3, turn, k3, turn, p3, turn, k3tog.

Row 1 (RS) Knit.

Row 2 and all WS rows Purl.

Row 3 K1,*MB, k5; rep from *, end k1.

Row 5 Knit.

Row 7 K4, *MB, k5; rep from *, end k3.

Row 8 Purl.

Rep rows 1–8.

247 bobble block

(multiple of 15 sts)

MB (make bobble) [K1, p1] twice in st, pass 2nd, 3rd, and 4th st over first st.

Rows 1, 3, 5, and 7 (RS) K5, *k1, [p1, k1] twice, p5, k5; rep from * to last 10 sts, k1, [p1, k1] twice, p 5.

Rows 2, 4, and 6 K5, k1, [p1, k1] twice, *p5, k5, k1, [p1, k1] twice; rep from *, end p5.

Rows 8 and 9 Knit.

Row 10 Purl.

Row 11 *K2, MB, k2; rep from * to end.

Row 12 Purl.

Rows 13 and 14 Knit.

Rep rows 1–14.

246

247

248 eyelets and bobbles

(multiple of 10 sts)

DVD (double vertical dec)

Sl next 2 sts to RH needle as if to k2tog, k next st, pass 2 slipped sts over k1.

MB (make bobble)

K into front, back, front and back of st to make 4 sts in one, turn, p4, turn, k2tog twice, turn, p2tog, turn, place st back on RH needle.

Row 1 (RS) Knit.

Row 2 and all WS rows Purl.

Row 3 * K5, yo, SKP, p1, k2tog, yo; rep from * to end.

Row 5 *K6, yo, DVD, yo, k1; rep from * to end.

Row 7 *K7, MB, k2; rep from * to end.

Row 9 Knit.

Row 11 *Yo, SKP, k1, k2tog, yo, k5; rep from * to end.

Row 13 *K1, yo, DVD, yo, k6; rep from * to end.

Row 15 *K2, MB, K7; rep from * to end.

Row 16 Purl.

Rep rows 1–16.

248

249 nosegay pattern

(worked over 12 sts)

MB (make bobble)

[K1, p1] twice in next st, turn, p4, turn, k4, turn, [p2tog] twice, turn, k2tog.

RC (right cross)

Sl 1 to cn and hold to *back*, k1, k1 from cn.

LC (left cross)

Sl 1 to cn and hold to *front*, k1, k1 from cn.

RPC (right purl cross)

Sl 1 to cn and hold to *back*, k1, p1 from cn.

LPC (left purl cross)

Sl 1 to cn and hold to *front*, k1, p1 from cn.

Preparation row (WS) K5, p2, k5.

Row 1 P4, RC, LC, p4.

Row 2 K3, LPC, p2, RPC, k3.

Row 3 P2, RPC, RC, LC, LPC, p2.

Row 4 K1, LPC, k1, p4, k1, RPC, k1.

Row 5 RPC, p1, RC, k2, LC, p1, LPC.

Row 6 P1, k2, p1, k1, p2, k1, p1, k2, p1.

Row 7 MB, p1, RPC, p1, k2, p1, LPC, p1, MB.

Row 8 [K2, p1] twice, [p1, k2] twice.

Row 9 P2, MB, p2, k2, p2, MB, p2.

Row 10 K5, p2, k5.

Rep rows 1–10.

249

250 bouquets

(multiple of 12 sts plus 7)

MB (make bobble)

K into front and back of next st twice, sl 4 sts back to LH needle, k2tog twice, sl 2nd st on RH needle over first st.

Rows 1, 3 and 5 (RS) K1, *wyif sl 5, k7; rep from *, end last rep k1.

Row 2 and all WS rows Purl.

Row 7 K3, *insert RH needle from below under 3 loose strands on RS of work and k next st (hook 3 strands), k11; rep from *, end last rep k3.

Row 9 K3, *MB, k11; rep from *, end last rep k3.

Row 11 K2, *[MB, k1] twice, k8; rep from *, end last rep k1.

Row 13 K1, *[MB, k1] 3 times, wyif sl 5 , k1; rep from *, end last rep [MB, k1] 3 times.

Row 15 K2, *[MB, k1] twice, k1, sl 5 wyif, k2; rep from *, end [MB, k1] twice, k1.

Row 17 K3, *MB, k3, wyif sl 5, k3; rep from *, end MB, k3.

Row 19 K9, *hook 3 strands as in row 7, k11; rep from *, end k9.

Row 21 K9, *MB, k11; rep from *, end rep k9.

Row 23 K8, *[MB, k1] twice, k8; rep from *, end k7.

Row 25 K7, *[MB, k1] 3 times, k6; rep from * to end.

Row 27 Rep row 23.

Row 29 Rep row 21.

Row 30 Purl.

Rep rows 1–30.

250

251 lily of the valley

(worked over 25 sts)

MB (make bobble)

K 5 sts in next st by [k1, k1 tbl] twice, k1, then pass 5th, 4th, 3rd and 2nd sts over first st.

Row 1 and all WS rows K1, p23, k1.

Row 2 P1, ssk, k6, [yo, k1] twice, SK2P, [k1, yo] twice, k6, k2tog, pl.

Row 4 P1, ssk, k5, yo, k1, yo, k2, SK2P, k2, yo, k1, yo, k5, k2tog, p1.

Row 6 P1, ssk, k4, yo, k1, yo, MB, k2, SK2P, k2, MB, yo, k1, yo, k4, k2tog, p1.

Row 8 P1, ssk, k3, yo, k1, yo, MB, k3, SK2P, k3, MB, yo, k1, yo, k3, k2tog, p1.

Row 10 P1, ssk, k2, yo, k1, yo, MB, k4, SK2P, k4, MB, yo, k1, yo, k2, k2tog, p1.

Row 12 P1, ssk, [k1, yo] twice, MB, k5, SK2P, k5, MB, [yo, k1] twice, k2tog, p1.

Row 14 P1, ssk, yo, k1, yo, MB, k6, SK2P, k6, MB, yo, k1, yo, k2tog, p1.

Rep rows 1–14.

252 eyelet leaf and bobble pattern

(worked over 23 sts)

MB (make bobble)

K into front, back, front, back and front of st, turn; p2tog, p1, p2tog, turn; k3 tog.

Row 1 (RS) K3, k2tog, k3, yo, p7, yo, k3, ssk, k3.

Row 2 and all WS rows P8, k7, p8.

Row 3 K2, k2tog, k3, yo, k1, p3, MB , p3, k1, yo, k3, ssk, k2.

Row 5 K1, k2tog, k3, yo, k2, p2, MB, p1, MB, p2, k2, yo, k3, ssk, k1.

Row 7 K2tog, k3, yo, k3, p3, MB, p3, k3, yo, k3, ssk.

Row 8 P8, k7, p8.

Rep rows 1–8.

251

252

253 bell stitch

(beg as multiple of 6 sts and end as multiple of 7 sts plus 6)

Row 1 (RS) Purl.

Row 2 Knit.

Row 3 P6, *cast on 8 sts, p6; rep from * to end.

Rows 4 and 6 K6, *p8, k6; rep from * to end.

Row 5 P6, *k8, p6; rep from * to end.

Row 7 P6, *ssk, k4, k2tog, p6; rep from * to end.

Row 8 K6, *p6, k6; rep from * to end.

Row 9 P6, *ssk, k2, k2tog, p6; rep from * to end.

Row 10 K6, *p4, k6; rep from * to end.

Row 11 P6, *ssk, k2tog, p6; rep from * to end.

Row 12 K6, *p2, k6; rep from * to end.

Row 13 P6, *k2tog, p6; rep from * to end.

Row 14 K6, *p1 tbl, k6; rep from * to end.

Row 15 P6, *k1 tbl, p6; rep from * to end.

Rep rows 14 and 15.

253

254 eye of lynx

(multiple of 8 sts plus 6)

Note Sts are decreased on rows 8 and 18, then increased back to original number on rows 9 and 19.

Rows 1 and 3 (WS) Knit.

Rows 2 and 4 Purl .

Rows 5 and 7 P5, *p1, wyif sl 2, p5; rep from *, end p1.

Rows 6 and 10 K1, *k5, wyib sl 2, k1; rep from *, end k5.

Row 8 K1, *SKP, yo, k2tog, k1, wyib sl 2, k1; rep from *, end SKP, yo, k2tog, k1.

Row 9 P2, p in front and back of next yo, p1, *p1, wyif sl 2, p2, p in front and back of next yo, p1; rep from *, end p1.

Rows 11 and 13 Knit.

Rows 12 and 14 Purl.

Rows 15 and 17 P2, wyif sl 2, p1, *p5, wyif sl 2, p1; rep from *, end p1.

Rows 16 and 20 K1, *k1, wyib sl 2, k5; rep from *, end last rep k2.

Row 18 K1, *k1, wyib sl 2, k1, SKP, yo, k2tog; rep from *, end k1, wyib sl 2, k2.

Row 19 P2, wyif sl 2, p1, *p1, p in front and back of next yo, p2, wyif sl 2, p1; rep from *, end p1.

Rep rows 1–20.

254

255 tuck stitch

(multiple of 4 sts plus 3)

Note When working pat st, sl all sts purlwise.

Row 1 (RS) K2, p1, *yo, p4; rep from * to last 4 sts, end yo, p2, k2.

Row 2 K3, *yarn to front of work, sl 1, drop the yo of preceding row off needle, yarn to back of work over RH needle (making a yo), k3; rep from * to end.

Row 3 K2, p1, *with yarn at front of work, sl both the yo and the sl-st of preceding row, yarn to back of work over needle and to front again (making a yo), p3; rep from *, end last rep p1, k2.

Row 4 K3, *yarn to front of work, sl the 2 yo's and the sl-st of preceding rows, yarn to back of work over needle (making a yo), k3; rep from * to end.

Row 5 K2, p1, *with yarn at front of work, sl the 3 yo's and the sl-st of preceding rows, yarn to back of work over needle and to front again (making a yo), p3; rep from *, end last rep p1, k2.

Row 6 K3, *yarn to front of work, insert RH needle from behind under the bundle of 4 yo strands (but not the sl-st) and purl these strands all tog, removing them from LH needle but leaving the sl-st behind on LH needle; then knit the sl-st; then insert the LH needle under the 4 yo strands and purl them tog again, k3; rep from * to end.

Row 7 K2, *k2tog, p1, SKP, p1; rep from *, end last rep k2.

Row 8 Knit.

Rep rows 1–8.

255

256 bells and rib

(multiple of 5 sts plus 1)

Row 1 (RS) K1, *p4, k1; rep from * to end.

Row 2 P1, *k4, p1; rep from * to end.

Rows 3 and 4 Rep rows 1 and 2.

Row 5 K1, *p2, cast on 4 sts, p2, k1; rep from * to end.

Row 6 P1, *k2, p into front and back of each of 4 cast-on sts, k2, p1; rep from * to end.

Row 7 K1, *p2, SKP, k4, k2tog, p2, k1; rep from * to end.

Row 8 P1, *k2, p6, k2, p1; rep from * to end.

Row 9 K1, *p2, SKP, k2, k2tog, p2, k1; rep from * to end.

Row 10 P1, *k2, p4, k2, p1; rep from * to end.

Row 11 K1, *p2, SKP, k2tog, p2, k1; rep from * to end.

Row 12 P1, *k1, p2tog, p2tog tbl, k1, p1; rep from * to end.

Rep rows 3–12.

257 fan stitch

(worked over 15 sts)

Row 1 (RS) K2, [k1, yo] 10 times, k3 — 25 sts.

Row 2 K2, p2tog, p17, p2tog tbl, k2 — 23 sts.

Row 3 K2, SKP, k15, k2tog, k2 — 21 sts.

Row 4 K2, p2tog, p13, p2tog tbl, k2 — 19 sts.

Row 5 K2, SKP, k11, k2tog, k2 — 17 sts.

Row 6 K2, p2tog, p9, p2tog tbl, k2 — 15 sts.

Rep rows 1–6.

unusual

256

257

258 gothic windows

(multiple of 10 sts plus 4)

RT (right twist) K2tog and leave on LH needle, k the first st again, sl both sts off LH needle.

LT (left twist) With RH needle behind LH needle, skip first st and k the second st tbl, then k both sts tog tbl.

Row 1 (RS) P1, k4, *RT, LT, k1, ssk, yo, k3; rep from *, end RT, LT, k1, ssk, yo, k1, p1.

Row 2 K1, p8, *p1, p2tog, yo, p7; rep from *, end p1, p2tog, yo, p1, k1.

Row 3 P1, k3, *RT, k2, LT, k4; rep from *, end RT, k2, LT, k3, p1.

Row 4 K1, p to last st, k1.

Row 5 P1, k2, RT, *k4, LT, k2, RT; rep from *, end k4, LT, k2, p1.

Row 6 K1, p4, p2tog, yo, p2, *p6, p2tog, yo, p2; rep from *, end p4, k1.

Row 7 P1, k1, RT, k1, *ssk, yo, k3, LT, RT, k1; rep from *, end ssk, yo, k3, LT, k1, p1.

Rows 8, 10, 12 and 14 K3, p2, p2tog, yo, p2, *p2, k2, p2, p2tog, yo, p2; rep from *, end p2, k3.

Rows 9, 11 and 13 P3, k2, *ssk, yo, k4, p2, k2; rep from *, end ssk, yo, k4, p3.

Row 15 P1, k1, LT, k1, *ssk, yo, k3, RT, LT, k1; rep from *, end ssk, yo, k3, RT, k1, p1.

Row 16 Rep row 6.

Row 17 P1, k2, LT, *k4, RT, k2, LT; rep from *, end k4, RT, k2, p1.

Row 18 Rep row 4.

Row 19 P1, k3, *LT, k2, RT, k4; rep from *, end LT, k2, RT, k3, p1.

Row 20 Rep row 2.

Row 21 P1, k4, *LT, RT, k1, ssk, yo, k3; rep from *, end LT, RT, k1, ssk, yo, k1, p1.

Rows 22, 24 and 26 K1, p5, k2, p1, *p1, p2tog, yo, p4, k2, p1; rep from *, end p1, p2tog, yo, p1, k1.

Rows 23, 25 and 27 P1, k4, *k1, p2, k2, ssk, yo, k3; rep from *, end k1, p2, k2, ssk, yo, k1, p1.

Row 28 Rep row 22.

Rep rows 1–28.

258

259 entrelac

(multiple of 10 sts)

Note 1 Each rectangle is 10 sts and 20 rows.

Note 2 When picking up sts on WS, push RH needle from RS to WS and purl.

Note 3 After first repeat of step 2, sts will be picked up along side edge of rectangle instead of triangle.

Note 4 All binding off is done when step 2 or 3 is completed.

Preparation Step 1 *K2, turn, p2, turn, k3, turn, p3. Cont in this manner working one more st every RS row until 10 sts have been worked, leave on RH needle – one triangle complete. Rep from * across row.

Step 2 (WS) Inc 1 st by purling in the front and back of first st, p2tog, turn, k3, turn, inc 1 in first st, p1, p2tog, turn, k4. Cont in this manner, inc 1 st in first st, with 1 more p st between, then p2tog on every WS row until 10 sts are on RH needle. Leave sts on RH needle. **With WS facing, pick up and p10 sts along side edge of first triangle, sl last picked up sts back to LH needle and p2tog with first st of next triangle, *turn, k10, turn, p9, p2tog with first st of next triangle; rep from * until 10 sts of triangle have been worked. Leave on RH needle. Rep from ** across row. On side edge of last triangle, pick up and p9, turn, k9, turn, p7, p2tog, turn, k8. Cont in this manner, p2tog at end of every WS row until 1 st rem. Turn.

Step 3 (RS) K1 and pick up and k9 sts along edge of first half-rectangle, k1 from first rectangle, sl last st picked up over it, *turn, p10, turn, k9, sl 1, k1 from rectangle, psso; rep from * until all 10 sts from first rectangle have been worked and there are 10 sts on RH needle. Leave on RH needle. Pick up and k10 sts along side edge of next rectangle. Rep from * as for last rectangle across row. Rep steps 2 and 3.

Bind off

Note Use either bind-off method depending on last step worked.

Step 2 Bind Off Beg step 2 and end on k6 row, turn.

Next row (WS) P2tog, p3, p2tog, turn, k5, turn, p2tog, p2, p2tog, turn, k4, turn, p2tog, p1, p2tog, turn, k3, turn, p2tog twice, turn, k2, turn, p2tog – 1 st rem. *Pick up and p10 sts, turn, k11, turn, p2tog, p8, p2tog, turn, k10, turn, cont in this manner, dec 1 st at each side, end p3tog – 1 st rem. Rep from *, end last triangle as foll: on side edge, pick up and p9 sts, turn, k10, turn, p2 tog at beg and end of row. Cont in this manner, end p3tog.

Step 3 Bind Off Beg step 3 by picking up sts and end on p10, turn.

Next row (RS) Sl 1, k1, psso at beg of every RS row, AT SAME TIME, cont to work dec at end of row as per step 3. End last rep with sl, k2tog, psso.

259

260 garter stitch x's

(worked over 24 sts)

Note 1 X's are over a St st background.

Note 2 Garter stitch bands are knit on needle size that is 3 sizes smaller than St st background.

With larger needles, work in St st for desired length to beginning of bands, ending with a WS row.

Beg Pat Next row (RS) Sl 16 sts to holder, co 16 sts to RH needle. Continue in St st until piece measures 5"/12.5cm from beginning, end with a WS row.

Garter st bands

Next row (RS) With RS facing, smaller needles and separate ball of yarn, k4 sts from holder. Work in garter st on these 4 sts only for 5"/12.5cm, end with a WS row. Place sts on a holder.* Rep between *'s 3 times more. All sts have been worked from holder and there are 4 strips of garter st bands.

Attach bands

Next row (RS) With larger needles and 2nd band overlapping first band [k 1 st of 2nd band tog with next st on St st piece] 4 times, k6 sts from St st piece, cross first garter st band over 4th band, then cross 3rd band over 4th band, work sts from first and 4th band as foll: [k 1 st of first band, 1 st of 4th band and next st on front piece tog] 4 times, k6 sts from St st piece, [k1 st of 3rd band tog with next st of St st piece] 4 times.

260

261 alternating brioche

(over an even number of sts)

K 1-b (knit 1 in row below)

Wyib, insert RH needle from front to back into center of stitch one row below stitch on LH needle. Knit the stitch, slipping off the top stitch.

Row 1 (WS) Knit.

Rows 2, 3, 4 and 5 *K1, k1-b; rep from * to end.

Rows 6, 7, 8 and 9 *K1-b, k1; rep from * to end.

Rep rows 2–9.

Note Work on different needle sizes for varying effects.

262 leaf pattern

(multiple of 10 sts plus 1)

Row 1 (RS) K2tog, k3, *yo, k1, yo, k3, SK2P, k3; rep from *, end yo, k1, yo, k3, SKP.

Row 2 and all WS rows Purl.

Row 3 K2tog, k2, *yo, k3, yo, k2, SK2P, k2; rep from *, end yo, k3, yo, k2, SKP.

Row 5 K2tog, k1, *yo, k5, yo, k1, SK2P, k1; rep from *, end yo, k5, yo, k1, SKP.

Row 7 K2tog, *yo, k7, yo, SK2P; rep from *, end yo, k7, yo, SKP.

Row 9 K1, *yo, k3, SK2P, k3, yo, k1; rep from * to end.

Row 11 K2, *yo, k2, SK2P, k2, yo, k3; rep from *, end yo, k2.

Row 13 K3, *yo, k1, SK2P, k1, yo, k5; rep from *, end yo, k3.

Row 15 K4, *yo, SK2P, yo, k7; rep from *, end yo, k4.

Row 16 Rep row 2.

unusual

261

262

263 checkerboard

(multiple of 22 sts plus 4)

Row 1 (RS) K1, wyif sl 2, *k2, wyif sl 2, k1, wyif sl 2, k2, wyif sl 2; rep from *, end k1.

Row 2 K1, *wyib sl 2, p2, wyib sl 2, p1, wyib sl 2, p2; rep from * to last 3 sts, end wyib sl 2, k1.

Row 3 Knit.

Rows 4, 8 and 12 K1, *wyib sl 2, [k1, p1] 4 times, k1, wyib sl 2, k9; rep from * to last 3 sts, end wyib sl 2, k1.

Rows 5, 9 and 13 K1, wyif sl 2, *p9, wyif sl 2, [p1, k1] 4 times, p1, wyif sl 2; rep from *, end k1.

Rows 6, 10 and 14 K1, *p2, [k1, p1] 5 times, p1, k9; rep from * to last 3 sts, end p2, k1.

Rows 7 and 11 K3, *p9, k2, [p1, k1] 5 times, k1; rep from *, end k1.

Row 15 Knit.

Row 16 Rep row 2.

Row 17 Rep row 1.

Row 18 K1, purl to last st, k1.

Rows 19, 23 and 27 K1, wyif sl 2, *[p1, k1] 4 times, p1, wyif sl 2, p9, wyif sl 2; rep from *, end k1.

Rows 20, 24 and 28 K1, *wyib sl 2, p9, wyib sl 2, k1, [p2tog, yo] 3 times, p1, k1; rep from * to last 3 sts, end wyib sl 2, k1.

Rows 21, 25 and 29 K3, *[p1, k1] 5 times, k1, p9, k2; rep from *, end k1.

Rows 22 and 26 K1, *p13, [k1, p1] 4 times, k1; rep from *, end p2, k1.

Row 30 K1, purl to last st, k1.

Rep rows 1–30.

263

(worked over 32 sts dec to 2 sts)

Note 1 Directions are for pleat only. Pleats may be added to any garment by casting on an additional 32 sts for each pleat.

Note 2 Hole formed by 6 bound-off sts at top of pleat can be sewn closed after piece is complete.

Row 1 (RS) Wyib sl 1, k7, p1, k14, p1, k7, wyib sl 1.

Row 2 and all WS rows Purl, slipping p sts of previous row wyib.

Rows 3 and 5 Rep row 1.

Row 7 Sl 1 Wyib, k4, k2tog, place marker, k1, p1, k1, ssk , k8, place marker, k2tog, k1, p1, k1, ssk, k4, wyib sl 1.

Rows 9 and 11 Wyib sl 1, k6, p1, k12, p1, k6, wyib sl 1.

Row 13 Wyib sl 1 wyib, k to 2 sts before marker, k2tog, sl marker, k1, p1, k1, ssk, k to 2 sts before next marker, k2tog, sl marker, k1, p1, k1, ssk, k to last st, wyib sl 1 . Cont in this way to dec 1 st each side of markers, every 6th row, until there are 12 sts.

Next row (RS) Sl 1, k2tog, p1, ssk, k2tog, p1, ssk, sl 1 – 8 sts. Work 3 rows even.

Next row K1, bind off center 6 sts – 2 sts rem.

Next row Purl.

265 diagonal eyelet brocade

(multiple of 12 sts plus 1)

SKP Slip 1, knit 1, pass slip st over.

S2KP Sl 2 sts tog as if to work k2tog, k1, pass the slipped sts over the k1.

Row 1 (RS) K1, *yo, SKP, k7, k2tog, yo, k1; rep from * to end.

Row 2 *P3, k7, p2; rep from *, end p1.

Row 3 K1, *yo, k1, SKP, k5, k2tog, k1, yo, k1; rep from * to end.

Row 4 *P4, k5, p3; rep from *, end p1.

Row 5 K1, *yo, k2, SKP, k3, k2tog, k2, yo, k1; rep from * to end.

Row 6 *P5, k3, p4; rep from *, end p1.

Row 7 K1, *yo, k3, SKP, k1, k2tog, k3, yo, k1; rep from * to end.

Row 8 *K2, [p4, k1] twice; rep from *, end k1.

Row 9 K1, *k1, yo, k3, S2KP, k3, yo, k2; rep from * to end.

Row 10 *K3, p7, k2; rep from *, end k1.

Row 11 K1, *k2, yo, k2, S2KP, k2, yo, k3; rep from * to end.

Row 12 *K4, p5, k3; rep from *, end k1.

Row 13 K1, *k3, yo, k1, S2KP, k1, yo, k4; rep from * to end.

Row 14 *K5, p3, k4; rep from *, end k1.

Row 15 K1, *k4, yo, S2KP, yo, k5; rep from * to end.

Row 16 Rep row 14.

Row 17 K1, *k3, k2tog, yo, k1, yo, SKP, k4; rep from * to end.

Row 18 Rep row 12.

Row 19 K1, *k2, k2tog, [k1, yo] twice, k1, SKP, k3; rep from * to end.

Row 20 Rep row 10.

Row 21 K1, *k1, k2tog, k2, yo, k1, yo, k2, SKP, k2; rep from * to end.

Row 22 *K2, p9, k1; rep from *, end k1.

Row 23 K1, *k2tog, k3, yo, k1, yo, k3, SKP, k1; rep from * to end.

Row 24 *K1, p4, k3, p4; rep from *, end k1.

Row 25 K1, k2tog, *k2, [yo, k3] twice, S2KP, k1; rep from * to last 2 sts, end SKP.

Row 26 Rep row 4.

Row 27 K1, k2tog, *k1, yo, k5, yo, k2, S2KP, k1; rep from * to last 2 sts, end SKP.

Row 28 Rep row 2.

Row 29 K1, k2tog, *yo, k7, yo, k1, S2KP, k1; rep from * to last 2 sts, end SKP.

Row 30 *P2, k9, p1; rep from *, end p1.

Row 31 K2tog, *yo, k9, yo, S2KP; rep from * to last 2 sts, end yo, SKP.

Row 32 Rep row 30.

Rep rows 1–32.

265

approx — approximately

beg — begin; begins; beginning

cn — cable needle

cont — continue; continuing

dec — decrease; decreasing

inc — increase; increasing

k — knit

k-b; k1-b — knit stitch in row below

k2tog — knit two together

k3tog — knit three together

LH — left-hand

lp; lps — loop; loops

m1 — make one

m1 p-st — make one purl stitch

p — purl

pat; pats — pattern; patterns

p 1-b — purl stitch in row below
With the yarn at the front, insert the right needle from back to front into the center of the stitch one row below the stitch on the left needle. Purl this stitch. Slip the top stitch off the left needle without working it.

pm — place marker

psso — pass slip stitch over

p2tog — purl two together

p3tog — purl three together

rem — remain; remaining

rep — repeat

RH — right-hand

RS — right side

SKP — slip one, knit one, pass slip stitch over

sl — slip

sm — slip marker

ssk — slip, slip, knit

st; sts — stitch; stitches

St st — stockinette stitch

tbl — through back loop

tog — together

WS — wrong side

wyib — with yarn in back

wyif — with yarn in front

yo — yarn over

yo twice; yo2 — yarn over two times

Yarn overs

1. Between two knit stitches

Bring the yarn from the back of the work to the front between the two needles. Knit the next stitch, bringing the yarn to the back over the right needle as shown.

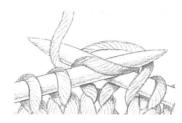

2. Between two purl stitches

Leave the yarn at the front of the work. Bring the yarn to the back over the right needle and to the front again as shown. Purl the next stitch.

3. Between a knit and a purl stitch

Bring the yarn from the back to the front between the two needles, then to the back over the right needle and to the front again as shown. Purl the next stitch.

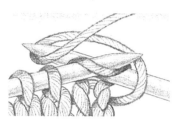

4. Between a purl and a knit stitch

Leave the yarn at the front of the work. Knit the next stitch, bringing the yarn to the back over the right needle as shown.

5. At the beginning of a knit row

Keep the yarn at the front of the work. Insert the right needle knitwise into the first stitch on the left needle. Bring the yarn over the right needle to the back and knit the next stitch, holding the yarn over with your thumb if necessary.

6. At the beginning of a purl row

To work a yarn over at the beginning of a purl row, keep the yarn at the back of the work. Insert the right needle purlwise into the first stitch on the left needle. Purl the stitch.

7. Multiple yarn overs

a. For multiple yarn overs (two or more), wrap the yarn around the needle as for a single yarn over, then wrap the yarn around the needle once more (or as many times as indicated). Work the next stitch on the left needle.

b. Alternate knitting and purling into the multiple yarn over on the subsequent row, always knitting the last stitch on a purl row and purling the last stitch on a knit row.

as foll Work the instructions that follow.

end last rep After completing a full repeat of a pattern and not enough stitches remain to complete another repeat, end the pattern repeat as directed.

hold to front (back) of work A term usually referring to stitches placed on a cable needle that are held to the front (or the back) of the work as it faces you.

k the knit sts and p the purl sts (as they face you) A phrase used when a pattern of knit and purl stitches has been established and will continue for a determined length (such as ribbing). Work the stitches as they face you: Knit the knit stitches and purl the purl stitches.

k the purl sts and p the knit sts: A phrase used when a pattern of knit and purl stitches will alternate on the following row or rows (such as in a seed stitch pattern). Work the stitches opposite of how they face you: Purl the knit stitches and knit the purl stitches.

knitwise (or as to knit) Insert the needle into the stitch as if you were going to knit it.

m1 Make one knit stitch as follows: Insert left needle from front to back under horizontal strand between stitch just worked and next stitch on left needle. Knit this strand through the back loop.

m1 p-st Make one purl stitch as follows: Insert left needle from front to back under horizontal strand between stitch just worked and next stitch on left needle. Purl this strand through the back loop.

multiple of . . . sts Used when working a pattern. The total number of stitches should be divisible by the number of stitches in one pattern repeat.

multiple of . . . sts plus . . . Used when working a pattern. The total number of stitches should be divisible by the number of stitches in one pattern repeat, plus the extra stitches (added only once).

next row (RS), or (WS) The row following the one just worked will be a right side (or wrong side) row.

place marker(s) Slide a stitch marker either onto the needle (where it is slipped every row) or attach it to a stitch, where it remains as a guide.

preparation row A row that sets up the stitch pattern but is not part of the pattern repeat.

purlwise Insert the needle into the stitch as if you were going to purl it.

rep from *, end . . . Repeat the instructions that begin at the asterisk as many times as you can work full repeats of the pattern, then end the row as directed.

rep from * to end Repeat the instructions that begin at the asterisk, ending the row with a full repeat of the pattern.

rep . . . times more Repeat a direction the designated number of times (not counting the first time you work it).

right side (or RS) Usually refers to the surface of the work that will face outside when the garment is worn.

row 2 and all WS (even-numbered) rows A term used when all the wrong-side or even-numbered rows are worked the same.

SKP On RS, slip one stitch. Knit next stitch and pass slip stitch over knit stitch. On WS, slip next two stitches knitwise. Slip these two stitches back to left needle without twisting them and purl them together through the back loops.

sk2p On RS, slip one stitch, knit two stitches together. Pass slipped stitch over two stitches knit together. On WS, slip two stitches to right needle as if knitting two together. Slip next stitch knitwise. Slip all stitches to left needle without twisting them. Purl these three stitches together through back loops.

slip marker To keep the stitch marker in the same position from one row to the next, transfer it from one needle to the other as you work each row.

ssk On RS, slip next two stitches knitwise. Insert tip of left needle into fronts of these two stitches and knit them together. On WS, slip one stitch, purl one stitch, then pass slip stitch over purl stitch.

stockinette stitch Knit every right-side row and purl every wrong-side row.

work to end Work the established pattern to the end of the row.

acknowledgments

Special thanks to:

The Knitters:

Lisa Buccellato

Jeannie Chin

Victoria Hilditch

Charlotte Parry

And also:

Karen Greenwald

Veronica Manno

Michelle Wiener

Claire Hilditch

Maria Gerbino

All yarn provided by Lana Grossa

Lana Grossa/Unicorn Books & Craft, Inc.,

1338 Ross Street

Petaluma, CA, 94954

www.lanagrossa.de

Dist. in the US by Unicorn Books & Crafts

www.unicornbooks.com

Knitting needles on cover provided by Lantern Moon.

Lantern Moon knitting needles are currently available in 4 distinct wood varieties.

Made entirely by hand, they are the perfect tool for knitters. The design detail and handfinishing

makes these needles as wonderful to work with as they are beautiful. Visit Lantern Moon online at

www.lanternmoon.com.